Cambridge assignments i

INVESTIGATING MUSICAL STYLES

ROY BENNETT

CAMBRIDGE
UNIVERSITY PRESS

Contents

* Indicates items not on the
accompanying cassettes.
Regrettably, permission could
not be obtained to include
certain tracks.

The variety of musical styles

When a composer creates a piece of music, she or he is working with several important musical elements – what we might call the basic 'ingredients' of music. These include:

melody •	rhythm •	harmony •	timbre •	texture

Also essential, and underlying all music, is:

form

This is the overall structure of the music, the way in which it is shaped and built up to form a balanced whole.

Other important factors which the composer relies on to achieve the overall effect and impact of the composition include:

tempo – speed; **dynamics** – varying degrees of loud and soft; and **expression**.

We use the word **style** mainly to describe the characteristic ways in which composers – of different times, and in different parts of the world – combine and present these basic ingredients in their music.

In some types and styles of music, all these ingredients may be apparent. In others, only some of them are present. For example, early Medieval music, and much of the music of Eastern cultures, makes no use of harmony. And in some 20th-century compositions there may be no melody to speak of.

It is the special way in which these musical ingredients are treated, balanced, combined, and presented which brings to any composition the distinctive 'flavour' or style of its period in history, and perhaps also its geographical location – at the same time providing characteristic 'fingerprints' as clues by which we may identify the musical style of individual composers.

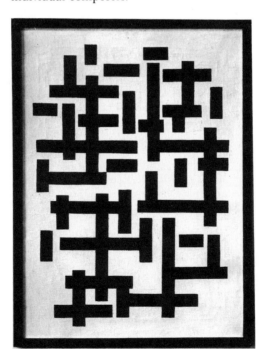

'Composition in Black and White' by the Dutch painter, Theo van Doesburg

We can divide the history of Western music into separate periods of time. And broadly speaking, each of these may be identified by its own characteristic musical style. Of course, a style does not change abruptly overnight. It is a gradual process, and different styles may overlap so that a 'new' style emerges from within the 'old'.

The music of the earliest period, lasting until about the middle of the 15th century, is generally described as Medieval. The music of the other five important periods may be described as:

Renaissance music	*c.*1450 – 1600
Baroque music	1600 – 1750
Classical music	1750 – 1810
19th-century Romanticism	1810 – 1910
20th-century music	1900 onwards

Before listening in detail to pieces of music from each of these periods, let us investigate five basic ingredients of music – illustrated in a variety of musical styles, from different periods and from various parts of the world.

MELODY

To many listeners, **melody** is the most important ingredient in a piece of music. Basically, a melody is a series of notes of varying pitches, organized and shaped to make musical sense to the listener. Also usually involved is the duration (long or short) of the various notes in relation to each other.

However, reaction to a melody is a very personal matter. What may make musical sense to one listener may be merely a meaningless jumble of notes to another. And what one person admires as an interesting or even magically expressive melody may leave someone else totally unmoved.

Here are some characteristic features of a melody:

- its *contour* or *shape*: the rise-and-fall of the notes, the way in which – now upwards, now downwards – they curve along in musical space and time;
- its *range* (lowest note to highest note): narrow, medium, or wide;
- whether it moves mainly by *step*, or by *leap*, or by a mixture of both;
- the type of *scale* on which its notes are based: major, minor, perhaps a mode, or some other type of scale;
- its *structure* and *phrasing* – which may involve repetition and/or variation of distinctive note-patterns.

Many melodies have survived mainly because they are easy to remember, and perhaps easy to sing, whistle or hum.

Listen to the famous English folk-melody, 'Greensleeves', which is more than 400 years old. It has four phrases, and is structured in binary form (in two sections: A, and B). The melody, printed overleaf, is based on the notes of the Dorian mode; you can hear what this mode sounds like by playing from D to D on only the white notes of the piano.

Dorian mode

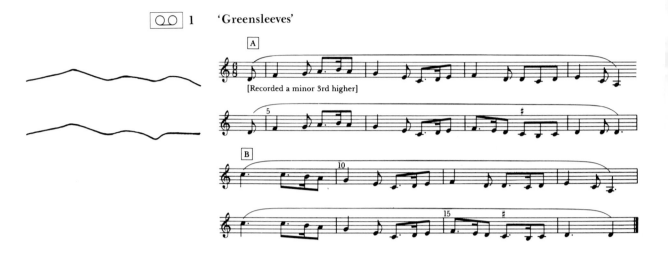

1 'Greensleeves'

[Recorded a minor 3rd higher]

Assignment 1

1 On the left, above, you can see the melodic shapes of the first two phrases (section A) of 'Greensleeves'. How are they similar? How are they different?

2 Listen again to 'Greensleeves', and make your own drawings of the melodic shapes of the last two phrases (section B) of the melody.

A melody may move mainly by step, and perhaps within a fairly narrow range:

2 'Panorama' from the ballet, *The Sleeping Beauty*, by Tchaikovsky

p [accompaniment in ⁶⁄₈]

Or, a melody may move mainly by leap, perhaps covering a fairly wide range:

3 **Symphony No. 4 in E minor (first movement) by Brahms**

Most melodies, however, move by a balanced mixture of step and leap (and perhaps also include repeated notes). Listen to a Minuet by Haydn. When the printed music ends, the recording continues. Then use your ears only to tell when the melody moves by step, and when by leap.

4   **Minuet from the 'Surprise' Symphony (No. 94 in G) by Haydn**

Assignment 2

1 What is the range (lowest note to highest note) of Tchaikovsky's melody (page 6)? What is the range of Brahms's melody?
2 Draw the melodic shape of the first 8 bars of these two melodies.
3 Listen again to the Minuet by Haydn. Note down bars from the printed music where, for more than two bars running:
   (a) the melody moves only by step;   (b) the melody moves only by leap;
   (c) the same short note-pattern is repeated, bar after bar.

Assignment 3

Compose a melody of your own, using a balanced mixture of step and leap.

The melody of 'Greensleeves' is based on a **mode** (the Dorian mode). The melodies by Tchaikovsky and Haydn are built from the notes of the **major scale** (G major, in both cases). Brahms structures his melody from the notes of the **minor scale** (E minor). Melodies may be built from other types of scale.

One of these is the **pentatonic** (five-note) **scale**, which is used in much European folk-music, especially Scottish (an example is the well-known melody, 'Auld Lang Syne'). Types of pentatonic scale form the basis of the musical styles of many other cultures - for example, China, Japan, Thailand, Indonesia, and parts of Africa.

5   Listen to part of a piece called *Nogkhao*, from Thailand. (A nogkhao is a colourful bird which, like a parrot, is able to talk.) This is a traditional Thai folk-tune, based on this pentatonic scale:

The music is played on typical Thai instruments: a *sǭ ū* and a *sǭ duang*, both two-string instruments played with a bow; a *jakhē*, which is a three-string zither plucked with an ivory plectrum; and *ching*, small hand cymbals made of thick metal.

jakhē

Some composers of the late 19th century and the 20th century have built melodies from the **whole-tone scale**. This consists of six notes only, a whole tone apart, spread equally across the octave. The fact that this scale contains no semitones, and no perfect 5ths or perfects 4ths, brings a vague, shifting, mysterious quality to the music.

One composer who made particular use of the whole-tone scale was Debussy. Listen to the beginning of his piece called 'Cloches à travers les feuilles' (Bells heard through the leaves) from his second set of *Images* for piano, composed in Impressionist style (see page 82). Debussy bases the music on this whole-tone scale:

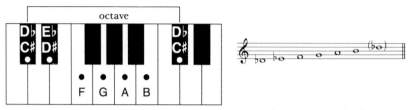

Another important scale is the **chromatic scale**, which divides the octave into twelve equal steps of a semitone each:

Listen to the cello melody which introduces Song No. 19, 'Serenade', from Schoenberg's set of songs called *Pierrot Lunaire* (Pierrot by Moonlight). In this melody, composed in atonal style (that is, not in any key), Schoenberg includes all twelve notes of the chromatic scale.

Assignment 4

1 Listen again to Schoenberg's melody. What kind of range does it have – wide, medium, or narrow?
2 Listen again. Do you think this melody moves mainly by step, mainly by leap, or with a balanced mixture of both?
3 What kind of mood do you think Schoenberg's melody presents?
4 It was suggested, on page 5, that reaction to a melody is a very personal matter. Listen once more to Schoenberg's melody. Does it have appeal for you? Why, do you think?

Assignment 5

Choose one of these types of scale:

| pentatonic scale | whole-tone scale | chromatic scale |

Compose a melody using the notes of your chosen scale.
In creating your melody, especially consider:
• shape and contour – the rise-and-fall of the melodic line;
• range – wide, medium, narrow;
• movement by step, or by leap;
• the most suitable note for your melody to end on.
Sing your melody, or perform it on a suitable instrument, and record it.

RHYTHM

The word **rhythm** is used to describe the various ways in which a composer groups together musical sounds, mainly with regard to *duration* (the lengths of different sounds, long or short, in relation to each other) and also *stress* or *accent*. Usually, going along in the background (either heard, or merely felt) there will be a pattern of regular **beats** – the steady 'pulse' or 'heart-beat' of the music, against which the ear measures rhythm.

Some beats carry a stronger accent than others. And so we sense that the beats are grouped into equal units – called **bars** – forming a repeating pattern made up either of twos, or threes, or fours. This gives us the **time**, or **metre**, of the music. The first beat of a bar usually carries the strongest accent:

• Duple metre	(2 beats to a bar)	| ONE two | ONE two
• Triple metre	(3 beats to a bar)	| ONE two three | ONE two three
• Quadruple metre	(4 beats to a bar)	| ONE two Three four | ONE two Three four

Notice that in quadruple time or metre (four beats to a bar) there are two accented beats – a strong accent on the first beat, a lesser accent on the third beat.

The repeating beat-pattern of any metre serves as a steady framework. Against this framework, rhythm – with its own accents, and varied note lengths – may flow freely.

The accents of a rhythmic melody may mainly coincide with the accents of the metre, as in this melody by Bizet:

8 **'Smugglers' March' from the opera, *Carmen*, by Bizet**

Now listen to a waltz melody by Tchaikovsky. Notice how the accents of the melody often do *not* coincide with the accents of the three-beat metre.

9 **'Waltz' from the ballet, *Swan Lake*, by Tchaikovsky**

[melody repeated, an octave higher, with woodwind decoration]

9

This interesting, and often exciting, rhythmic effect is known as **syncopation**. The composer deliberately alters what we *expect* to be the stress of the beats in the metre. And this gives Tchaikovsky's *Waltz* a tremendous 'swing'. A composer may create syncopation:

- by placing an accent on a weak beat;
- by placing an accent *between* the beats ('off' the beat);
- by placing a rest on a strong beat;
- by tying (holding on) over a strong beat;
- by combining two, or more, of the above effects.

Syncopation was an important feature of the style of ragtime, which originated in the USA towards the end of the 19th century. In a piano rag, the pianist plays a strongly syncopated melody with the right hand, above a steady beat marked out with the left hand. Listen to part of a piano rag by the American ragtime composer, Scott Joplin.

10 *Pine Apple Rag*   Scott Joplin (1868–1917)

[Note: Do not play this piece fast. It is never right to play Ragtime fast. *Composer.*]

Assignment 6   Listen again to the music by Tchaikovsky (page 9) and by Scott Joplin. Which of the above ways of creating syncopation does each composer use?

Music may have more than four beats to a bar - in which case each bar is really made up of some combination of two and three. For example, $\frac{5}{4}$ (five beats to a bar) may be stressed as:

| ONE two Three four five | or as: | ONE two three Four five |

Investigate pieces in different styles in $\frac{5}{4}$ time or metre, such as the second movement of Tchaikovsky's *Pathétique* Symphony, and Dave Brubeck's 'Take Five' (on his album with the same title).

In his *Chichester Psalms*, Leonard Bernstein makes exciting use of $\frac{7}{4}$ time (seven beats to a bar) in his setting of Psalm 100 ('Make a joyful noise . . .'), the dancing, bouncing seven-beat metre perfectly matching the mood of the words. Bernstein stresses the beats as:

11 | ONE two Three four Five six seven |

As another example of music with beats grouped in sevens, listen to a demonstration of an Indian *tala* (repeating rhythm cycle) played on a *mṛdaṅgam* - a south Indian double-headed barrel drum, combining treble and bass drums in one instrument. The music is introduced by Yehudi Menuhin. This particular south Indian tala is called *miśra cāpu*:

12 | ONE two three Four five Six seven |

13 **Assignment 7**   Listen to Dave Brubeck's 'Unsquare Dance' (from his album *Take Five*).
1 (a) How many beats to a bar has this music?
  (b) Does the metre ever change, or does it always remain the same?
  (c) Which instruments play rhythmically and freely against the
      framework of the metre?
2 Listen again, steadily counting out the beats. Then join in by crisply
  clapping only those beats you hear being clapped on the recording.
  Keep clapping, then also tap your foot on each beat in the pattern which
  is not clapped - marked by the *pizzicato* double bass. (When you reach
  the end, do you think you have earned Dave Brubeck's approval?)

Scott Joplin

11

Another exciting rhythmic effect is called **polyrhythm**, in which two or more different rhythms or metres are heard going along at the same time. Sometimes, the different rhythms strongly conflict against each other.

Listen to Ben Baddoo, born in Ghana but now based in Bristol, introducing a group of percussion instruments – some from the 'Ewe drum set' of Ghana, and some from other parts of the world. As the instruments join in one by one, each with its own rhythm, a complicated *polyrhythmic* music is built up in the dance and song styles of Ghana known as *kpanlogo* (this word can also mean 'having fun'!). You will hear the instruments enter in this order:

14

- single cowbell
- pair of cowbells (*gankogui*)
- *cabaça*, a gourd, covered with a network of beads, and shaken
- *gome* drum, square-shaped, from Cameroon
- *kaganu*, first drum of the Ewe set
- *kidi*, the brother of kaganu
- *congas*, drums from South America
- *sogo*, the big brother of kaganu
- talking drum (*donno*), from north Ghana

In the front: talking drum (donno) with drumstick, cowbell, cabaça; in the centre: the square-shaped gome drum; behind (left to right): kidi, two congas, atsimevu (not heard in the recording), sogo, and kaganu.

Assignment 8

1 Form a group of three or four musicians, each with a different percussion instrument. Each makes up a rhythm pattern (different from the other members in the group) lasting for one or two bars in $\frac{4}{4}$ time.

Practise your rhythms individually, steadily repeating your pattern over and over.

Then superimpose the rhythms – players enter one by one (at a distance of 4 or 8 bars) until all are playing. Continue playing, and listen carefully. Check for balance (are any too loud? should any play more loudly?) Make a recording; then listen to it, and discuss it.

2 Experiment with other metres: for example, $\frac{3}{4}$, $\frac{5}{4}$. Or with each person creating a repeating rhythm pattern in a *different* metre from the other members of the group.

HARMONY

Harmony is heard when two or more different notes are sounded at the same time, producing a chord. We use the word 'harmony' in two ways: to refer to the choice of notes which make up an individual chord; or, in a broader sense, to describe the overall flow or progression of chords throughout a composition.

Listen to a 12-bar blues progression (played three times) in the key of C major:

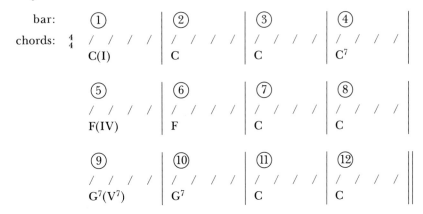

These are the chords which are used:

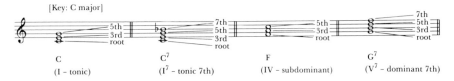

Chords are of two kinds:

- **concords**, in which the notes 'agree' with each other; and
- **discords**, in which (to a greater or lesser extent) certain notes 'disagree', or clash, creating an effect of restlessness and tension.

Play or listen to the following series of chords. The chords range from consonant, to more dissonant.

The first chord is built from a triad of A major: A–C♯–E (root, 3rd, 5th). This is in fact the only concord in this series of chords. All the others include four or more notes of different letter-names, and technically, all these are discords. For instance, the second chord in this series is a chord of the seventh: A–C–E–G (root, 3rd, 5th, 7th). And the third chord is a chord of the ninth: G–B♭–D–F–A (root, 3rd, 5th, 7th, 9th).

13

Assignment 9   Investigate three varied excerpts of music.

[□□] 16   The first, the 'magic bells tune' from Mozart's opera, *The Magic Flute* (1791), consists mainly of concords, but with some dominant sevenths. Is this music in a major key, or a minor key?

[□□] 17   The second excerpt, 'The Great Chorale' from *The Soldier's Tale* (1918) by Stravinsky, relies mainly on discords - but see if you notice any concords being sounded.

[□□] 18   The third excerpt is from Berg's opera, *Wozzeck* (1917–22). Here, the music consists entirely of discords, and at first, the harmony is in atonal style (not in any key, major or minor). But towards the end of the excerpt, though still making use of strong discords, the music definitely moves into a key (the key of D minor). See if you can tell when this happens.

TIMBRE   Each instrument has its own special sound-quality, or 'tone-colour'. The characteristic sound of a trumpet, for instance, makes it possible for us to recognize it immediately - to tell the difference between a trumpet and, say, a violin. We call this special sound-quality the **timbre** of an instrument.

A composer may **blend** similar timbres together - for instance, instruments of the string section of the orchestra. Listen to an example of this from

[□□] 19   Sibelius's symphonic poem, *Tapiola* (Tapio is the Finnish god of forests). In this excerpt, Sibelius blends low string sounds and high string sounds alternately and then combines them, with haunting harmonies.

A composer may combine instruments with similarly rich, dark timbres -

[□□] 20   as in another passage from *Tapiola*, where Sibelius blends together the timbres of these instruments, one group after the other:

low clarinets	low clarinets
bass clarinet	bass clarinet
bassoons	bassoons
double bassoon	double bassoon
low horns	violas
kettle drum roll	cellos
	double basses

Other instruments whose timbres blend particularly well together are members of the saxophone family. Listen, for example, to recordings by the Marcel Mule Saxophone Quartet, or the all-female saxophone quartet called The Fairer Sax.

A composer may choose to **contrast** the timbres of certain instruments so that the sounds stand out distinctively from one another - for instance, high-sounding instruments with bright, penetrating timbres, perhaps against a background of lower-sounding instruments whose timbres are darker, more sombre. An example is 'The Devil's Dance' from Stravinsky's *The Soldier's Tale*.

⟦▢⟧ 21 **Assignment 10** *The Soldier's Tale* is for six solo instruments and percussion. Stravinsky wanted to include 'the most representative instruments, in treble and bass, of the instrumental families'. As you listen to their contrasting timbres in 'The Devil's Dance', identify as many instruments as you can. Note down each one, naming the section of the orchestra to which it belongs.

Investigate examples of contrasting timbres from East Asian countries:

⟦▢⟧ 22 (1) A percussion ensemble from China, including the sounds of: two small bells struck against each other, tam-tam (a huge gong), the higher-pitched opera gong, wooden clappers, drums, cymbals, and the war-dance gong (the sound falls in pitch before dying away).

⟦▢⟧ 23 (2) An instrumental ensemble from Korea in an extract from music called *The Four Seasons*. The contrasting timbres you will hear include those of: *taegŭm* (transverse bamboo flute), *hyangp'iri* (double-reed wind instrument), *haegŭm* (2-string fiddle), *ajaeng* (7-string bowed zither), *kayagŭm* (23-string plucked zither), and percussion.

TEXTURE

Some pieces of music present a rather thin, sparse sound, perhaps producing an effect which is angular, or jagged. Other pieces present a rather dense sound – rich, smoothly flowing, perhaps rather complicated. To describe this aspect of music, we use the word **texture**, likening the way the sounds are woven together in a musical composition to the way in which the threads are woven in a piece of fabric.

Listen to two examples from the finale of Mahler's Symphony No. 5 in
C♯ minor, written for a large orchestra of more than a hundred players.

⟦▢⟧ 24 At the opening of the movement, the texture of the music is thin, light, sparse, and open – sometimes with just a single instrument heard. At the

⟦▢⟧ 25 end of the movement, the musical texture is rich, dense, complicated, massive – with the full orchestra involved.

There are four basic styles in which musical texture may be woven:

● **Monophonic texture:** the simplest kind of musical texture, consisting of a single melodic line (strand of melody) with no supporting harmonies – as in plainsong, many Medieval songs and dances, and much folk-music. The single melody may be performed by one musician, or several in unison, and may be accompanied by percussion instruments or a drone (one or more notes sustained or persistently repeated, usually in the bass).

⟦▢⟧ 26 Example: a Medieval dance of the 14th century called *La Manfredina*, played on viol, recorder, tabor, and tambourine.

Assignment 11 What changes happen in the music, halfway through this Medieval dance?

- **Homophonic** texture: a single melody is heard against a (usually) chordal accompaniment with basically the same rhythm moving in all the parts at the same time. This kind of musical texture may be described as 'melody-plus-accompaniment'.

27 Example: Mazurka in A minor, Opus 17 No. 4, by Chopin.

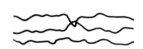

- **Polyphonic**, or **contrapuntal**, texture: consisting of two or more equally important melodic lines (strands of melody) weaving along together. Quite different melodies may be combined. Or the contrapuntal texture may be woven from just one musical idea with the voices or instruments entering one after another in *imitation*.

28 Example: a chorus from Handel's oratorio, *Messiah*: 'For unto us a child is born, unto us a son is given'. Two melodic lines weave along in counterpoint, presented in bars 1-6 by tenors and sopranos. Then, when altos and basses take over, the two melodic lines swap places in pitch – the higher line (which was sung by sopranos) is now heard *below* the other one.

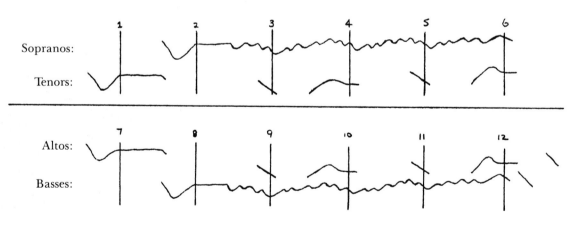

- **Heterophonic** texture: in this kind of musical texture, everyone performs – at the same time – different versions of the same melody. For instance, one voice or instrument performs a simple melody while another presents a more intricate, decorated version of it. Others may join in, presenting even more intricate versions of the melody, or perhaps a simplified version (presenting just a few important notes). This heterophonic style of performance is found in the folk-music of certain European countries, and in the music of Eastern cultures.

Examples:

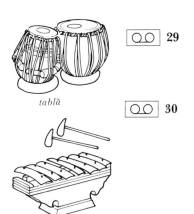

tablā

(1) 'Song of Mirabai' from India, in light classical style, sung in Hindi. A bamboo flute simultaneously plays a decorated version of the singer's melody. The accompaniment is provided by a pair of hand-played drums called *tablā*.

saron (metallophone)

(2) The *Legong* dance from Bali. This is played by a *gamelan* – an Indonesian instrumental ensemble made up mainly of metallophones, xylophones, various sizes of single gongs, gong-chimes (sets of gongs graded in size and pitch), and drums. A main 'fixed' melody is played in long notes by the lower-sounding instruments while, above and around it, other instruments improvise different versions of the same melody in various degrees of intricacy. For example, 12 seconds after the music begins, listen for this:

Gangsa (metallophone) players in a Balinese gamelan

Assignment 12   Listen to music by Benjamin Britten – the beginning of the first
Sea Interlude, called 'Dawn', from his opera *Peter Grimes*. Here is a plan of
this part of the piece showing the approximate elapsed timing at the start of
each small section. Sections 1 and 3 share a similar sound; and sections 2
and 4 share a similar sound.

0'00"	0'26"	0'39"	1'08"
1 violins and flutes; then clarinets, harp, violas, cymbal roll	2	3	4

Britten contrasts, in turn, two different kinds of musical *texture*, and also
instrumental *timbres*.

(a) What contrasts are there between the two textures – how are they
different?

(b) Describe the contrasts between the instrumental timbres you hear.

(c) Listen to the music again. How does Britten express in his music the
mood or atmosphere – and, in fact, any pictorial details – of 'on the
sea-shore at dawn'?

🔊 32 **Assignment 13**   Listen to the first four minutes or so of Stravinsky's symphonic poem,
The Song of the Nightingale, based on a story by Hans Christian Andersen
about a Chinese Emperor and two nightingales (a real one, and a
mechanical one). The music is scored for an orchestra made up of:

flute	4 horns	kettle drums	tambourine	2 harps
piccolo	3 trumpets	snare drum	cymbals	
2 oboes	3 trombones	triangle	bass drum	strings
2 clarinets	tuba	celesta	tam-tam	
2 bassoons		piano		

As you listen, notice how Stravinsky constantly changes the *texture* of the
music, and also the combinations of instrumental *timbres* – sometimes
blending them, often sharply contrasting them.

Here, with approximate timings, are a few of the main musical events to
listen out for:

0'00"   dense, complicated, busy texture; vivid, clashing timbres.

0'19"   texture still busy – but thinner, lighter, more open.

(Other changes of texture and timbre occur . . .)

1'24"   the real nightingale sings (which instrument portrays its song?).

2'14"   two brass instruments, alone (which ones?) – followed by a colourful
Chinese March.

To match the atmosphere of the story, Stravinsky often uses 'Chinese effects'
(especially at around 3'24"). Which kind of scale does he base his melody
on? Which particular instrumental timbres does he use at this point to bring
Chinese 'colour' to his music?

Renaissance Breakaway c.1450~1600

Renaissance means 'revival' or 'rebirth'. It is the name given to a period in European history when there was keen enthusiasm for the rebirth of learning, and for the revival of the artistic and cultural values of the ancient Greeks. It was also an age of scientific inquiry, of exploration and discovery - the time when Columbus and other famous explorers were making their great voyages of discovery, and important advances were being made in science and astronomy.

Winds of change were blowing - and these had great impact upon painters and architects, writers and composers. They now became more free to express themselves and enrich the lives of those around them.

Composers broke away from the restrictions of many of the devices and techniques of Medieval music, and began to use a freer, more expressive musical style. Music was still based upon the Medieval church modes, but these were gradually used with more freedom. Although some of the finest Renaissance music was composed for the Church, composers now took a keener interest in writing secular (non-sacred) pieces. These included many different types of song, and also pieces written for instruments independent of voices.

One of the most important Renaissance breakaways from Medieval style was in musical *texture*. A Medieval composer had tended to contrast the separate musical strands one against another, resulting at times in some crunching discords. A Renaissance composer aimed to blend the musical strands together - either by using a simple chordal style (homophonic texture), often structuring the music in clear-cut sections, or by writing in a contrapuntal (or polyphonic) style, weaving together the various strands of the music in a continuous, 'seamless' musical flow. But even when creating a contrapuntal texture, the Renaissance composer was becoming increasingly aware of harmony - the vertical framework of chords which supports the horizontal weaving of the counterpoint. Harmony became fuller and more expressive, and there was a greater concern with the treatment of discords.

Timechart: Renaissance composers

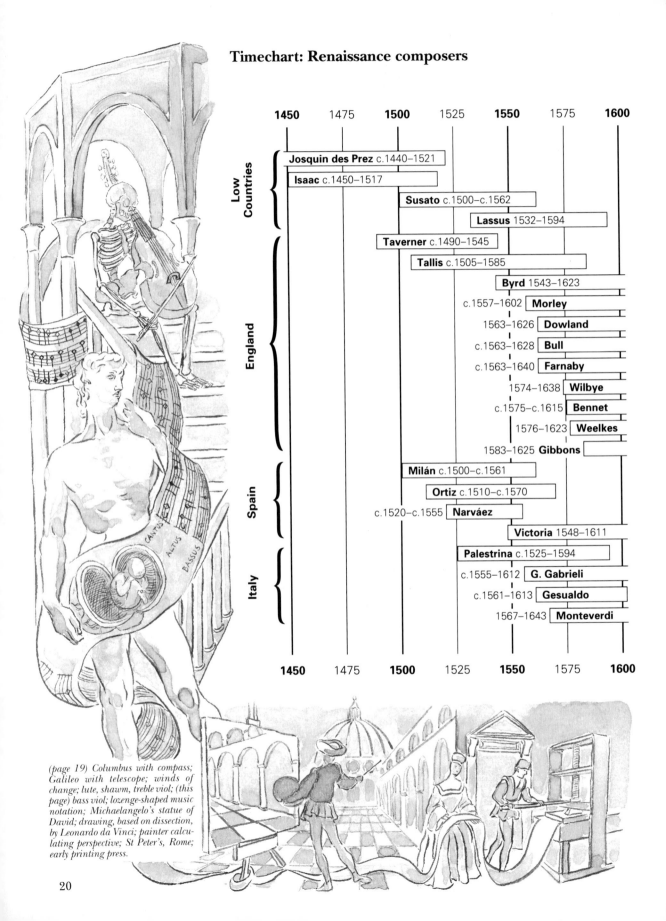

	1450	1475	1500	1525	1550	1575	1600

Low Countries
- **Josquin des Prez** c.1440–1521
- **Isaac** c.1450–1517
- **Susato** c.1500–c.1562
- **Lassus** 1532–1594

England
- **Taverner** c.1490–1545
- **Tallis** c.1505–1585
- **Byrd** 1543–1623
- c.1557–1602 **Morley**
- 1563–1626 **Dowland**
- c.1563–1628 **Bull**
- c.1563–1640 **Farnaby**
- 1574–1638 **Wilbye**
- c.1575–c.1615 **Bennet**
- 1576–1623 **Weelkes**
- 1583–1625 **Gibbons**

Spain
- **Milán** c.1500–c.1561
- **Ortiz** c.1510–c.1570
- c.1520–c.1555 **Narváez**
- **Victoria** 1548–1611

Italy
- **Palestrina** c.1525–1594
- c.1555–1612 **G. Gabrieli**
- c.1561–1613 **Gesualdo**
- 1567–1643 **Monteverdi**

	1450	1475	1500	1525	1550	1575	1600

(page 19) Columbus with compass; Galileo with telescope; winds of change; lute, shawm, treble viol; (this page) bass viol; lozenge-shaped music notation; Michaelangelo's statue of David; drawing, based on dissection, by Leonardo da Vinci; painter calculating perspective; St Peter's, Rome; early printing press.

Music to entertain Queen Elizabeth I

Listen to a five-part madrigal, '**All creatures now are merry-minded**', by the English composer, John Bennet. It is from a collection of madrigals called *The Triumphs of Oriana*, written by various English composers in honour of Elizabeth I, who was often called 'Oriana' in poetry. In the 16th century, 'triumph' was a name given to a Court tournament at which noblemen challenged each other and showed off their skills at jousting. So it has been suggested that some of the madrigals were performed at the two-day tournament which was held on the field below Windsor Castle on 17th/18th November 1593.

The recording on the cassette reconstructs a few moments of what might have taken place. First you will hear noises, then a fanfare followed by the madrigal. Most often, a madrigal would have been sung by unaccompanied solo voices. But as this performance takes place in the open air, and on an important occasion, typical instruments are used at times to support the voices. Sometimes you will hear a consort (group) of viols, sometimes an ensemble of cornetts and sackbuts, and sometimes all these instruments together.

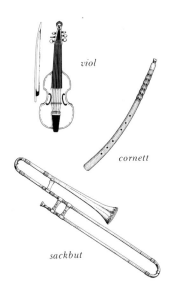

viol

cornett

sackbut

As you listen, notice how Bennet alternates two kinds of musical texture:
- **chordal style** (homophonic texture), with the voices mainly keeping rhythmically in step with each other; and
- **contrapuntal style** (polyphonic texture), often using **imitation** – one voice introduces a snatch of tune, then is immediately imitated, or copied, by another voice (for example, at 'the shepherds' daughters playing').

Bennet also, at times, uses another favourite technique, known as **word-painting** – vivid musical illustrations of the meaning of certain words. For example, at 'yond bugle' the voices really sound like bugles.

⟦◯◯⟧ 33

All creatures now are merry-minded.
→ The shepherds' daughters playing,
   The nymphs are fa-la-la-ing,
→ Yond bugle was well winded.
   At Oriana's presence each thing smileth.
   The flowers themselves discover;
   Birds over her do hover;
   Music the time beguileth.
   See where she comes with flowery garlands crownèd.
   Queen of all queens renownèd.
   Then sang the shepherds and nymphs of Diana:
   Long live fair Oriana.

Assignment 14

Listen to this Elizabethan madrigal two or three times more.
1 During which lines of the poem do the voices sing unaccompanied?
2 Pick out another example of *word-painting*. How does Bennet 'paint', or express, the idea in his music?
3 Are the following lines set in chordal style, or in contrapuntal style?
   (a) The nymphs are fa-la-la-ing,
   (b) See where she comes with flowery garlands crownèd.
   (c) Long live fair Oriana.

The Golden Age

Some of the finest Renaissance music was composed for the Church. The most typical forms were the Mass and the motet. The musical style is described as **choral polyphony** – contrapuntal music for one or more choirs, with several singers to each voice-part. Much of this music was intended to be sung **a cappella** (really 'in the style of the chapel', and so taken to mean choral music sung without instrumental accompaniment). The second half of the 16th century is sometimes called the 'Golden Age' of church music. Among the finest composers of the time were Palestrina (Italy), Lassus (Low Countries), Byrd (England), and Victoria (Spain).

Listen to the opening music, **Kyrie I**, of Palestrina's *Missa Brevis*, composed in 1570. Two words are sung again and again:

Kyrie eleison   Lord have mercy

The music is written in four voice-parts, perfectly blending together. Palestrina weaves the contrapuntal texture of his music from a single phrase of melody, which he uses in **imitation**. It is introduced by the altos, then taken up by other voice-groups one after another.

Assignment 15   (a) Does Palestrina plan this music in separate clear-cut sections, or does it flow continuously from beginning to end?

(b) The music is structured from a single phrase of melody, used in imitation. The first five imitational entries are marked on the score:
(1) altos;   (2) basses;   (3) trebles;   (4) tenors;   (5) basses again.
Which voice-groups enter with the melodic phrase when it is heard for the sixth, seventh, and eighth times?

(c) Which of the following match the mood, and the texture, of this music?
mood: light-hearted;   thoughtful;   tense;   calm and serene.
texture: smooth;   jerky and angular;   hesitant;   flowing.

(d) Which of these sing in the recording on the cassette?
The Manchester Boys' Choir   Huddersfield Choral Society
The Choir of St John's College, Cambridge   The King's Singers

The Glory of Venice

Choral music in a rather different style was being composed in Venice. At St Mark's Cathedral there were two organ lofts with galleries for singers and instrumentalists, set high up to left and right. So composers enjoyed writing music for two or more separate and contrasted groups of musicians. Pieces in this style are described as **polychoral** – music for more than one choir. A musical idea sounding from the left is answered by the same, or perhaps a different, idea from the right; and there are splendidly rich and powerful effects when the full forces are combined. The musical effect of this passing to and fro of musical ideas between the groups is called **antiphony**.

The texture of polychoral music is a mixture of chordal style and imitative counterpoint. And there is a mixture, too, of blending and contrasting – within each group the sounds might be blended, but there are contrasts of various kinds *between* the groups. For example, in:

- *pitch* – higher-pitched sounds against lower-pitched sounds;
- *dynamics* – the contrast of *piano* (soft) against *forte* (loud);
- *texture* – solo voices and/or instruments against massed groupings;
- *timbre* – brighter timbres (tone-colours) against darker, richer timbres.

St Mark's Cathedral, Venice

An example of a piece in polychoral style is Giovanni Gabrieli's motet, ***Angelus ad Pastores*** (1587), which would have been performed in St Mark's at Christmas time. Gabrieli writes this music for two six-part groups: Coro I, higher-pitched; Coro II, lower-pitched. *Coro* is Italian for 'choir', but the word may be applied to an ensemble made up of voices, or instruments, or both.

In the recording on the cassette, Coro I (on the left) consists of a six-part choir (SSAATB), and Coro II (right) consists of a male alto and five instruments (cor anglais and four bassoons).

Here are the words of this Christmas motet:

Angelus ad pastores ait:	The angel said to the shepherds:
annuncio vobis gaudium magnum;	I bring you tidings of great joy;
quia natus est vobis hodie	for unto you is born this day
Salvator mundi.	the Saviour of the world.
Alleluya.	Alleluya.
Gloria in excelsis Deo	Glory to God in the highest,
et in terra pax hominibus	and on earth, peace to men
bonae voluntatis.	of good will.
Alleluya.	Alleluya.

Gabrieli structures his motet in six contrasting sections of music. Here is a plan of the first three sections. ('Full' indicates where the full forces of Coro I and Coro II are combined.)

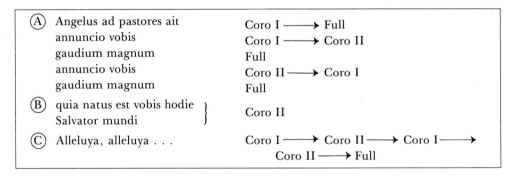

Assignment 16   Listen again to Gabrieli's polychoral motet. The passing to and fro of musical ideas between the groups is called *antiphony*. In which section or sections of the piece do you find these antiphonal effects are most noticeable?

Assignment 17   The plan given in the box on page 24 shows details of the first three sections of Gabrieli's motet, *Angelus ad Pastores*. Complete the plan by adding details for sections D, E, and F:

Ⓓ   Gloria in excelsis Deo
Gloria in excelsis Deo

Ⓔ   Et in terra pax hominibus
bonae voluntatis
et in terra pax hominibus
bonae voluntatis

Ⓕ   Alleluya, alleluya . . .
Alleluya, alleluya . . .

Assignment 18   In his motet, Gabrieli contrasts two groups of musicians. He also presents contrasts between the sections of music which structure the piece. Listen to the motet again.
1 How does section B present contrasts after the music of section A?
2 What contrasts does section C present after the music of A and B?
3 How is section D different from the other sections?

Assignment 19   Listen again to Kyrie I by Palestrina and to Gabrieli's motet. First note down these two headings:

Kyrie I from *Missa Brevis* by Palestrina	Motet: *Angelus ad Pastores* by Gabrieli

Then as you listen to each piece, list the characteristic features of the musical style, chosen from this box:

---

imitation used throughout   two contrasted groups   single mood and texture throughout

voices and instruments used   mood and texture change according to meaning of words

music structured in clear-cut sections   four-part choir   performed *a cappella*

use of physical space for musical effect   antiphony used   continuous 'seamless' flow of music

---

Renaissance music for instruments

During the 16th century, composers took a keener interest in writing music specially intended for instruments alone. These included dances, and pieces purely for playing and listening.

Many instrumental pieces, including dances, were structured upon a well-known bass-line and its framework of chords, which would be repeated throughout the piece. Here are four bass-lines, with their chord patterns, which were very popular with Renaissance composers:

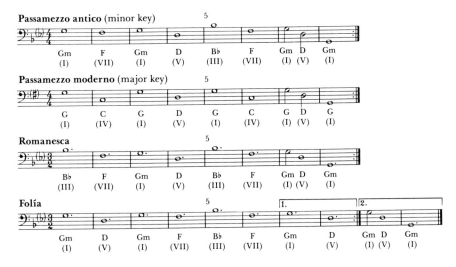

Passamezzo antico (minor key)

| Gm | F | Gm | D | Bb | F | Gm D | Gm |
| (I) | (VII) | (I) | (V) | (III) | (VII) | (I) (V) | (I) |

Passamezzo moderno (major key)

| G | C | G | D | G | C | G D | G |
| (I) | (IV) | (I) | (V) | (I) | (IV) | (I) (V) | (I) |

Romanesca

| Bb | F | Gm | D | Bb | F | Gm D | Gm |
| (III) | (VII) | (I) | (V) | (III) | (VII) | (I) (V) | (I) |

Folía

| Gm | D | Gm | F | Bb | F | Gm | D | Gm D | Gm |
| (I) | (V) | (I) | (VII) | (III) | (VII) | (I) | (V) | (I) (V) | (I) |

In each pattern, the chords in bar 7 might be altered slightly. And the bass-line might be filled in with other notes of shorter value.

Listen to a short **Passamezzo** by an anonymous Renaissance composer. The passamezzo (meaning 'step and a half') was a dance which became popular throughout Europe in the second half of the 16th century. This one is based on the *passamezzo antico* pattern (see above). The music is played by a shawm and two sackbuts.

shawm

sackbut

36

clavichord

In this short piece the pattern is played through twice only. Usually, to make the music longer, a string of variations would be played (often improvised) on the repeating bass-line and its chord pattern. Listen to a short set of variations by the Spanish composer, Narváez, on the *Romanesca* pattern. In Spain, it was known as **Guárdame las vacas** ('Watch over the cows for me'). The music is played on a clavichord, in which the strings are struck by metal tangents.

37 **Assignment 20**

As you listen to the music, follow the *Romanesca* pattern, above. (Narváez transposes it to a lower pitch.) The piece begins with the first variation on the pattern. How many variations do you hear altogether?

27

38 **Assignment 21**   Investigate a piece called ***The Antyck***, by another anonymous 16th-century composer. It is played on one of the most popular Renaissance instruments, the lute.

(a) The music is structured on one of the four bass-lines plus chord patterns on page 27. Which one is it?

(b) How many times is the pattern heard?

(c) As the pattern is repeated, is the music continually varied – or is it ever the same?

Assignment 22   Form a small group of musicians.

1 Choose a bass-line and its chord pattern from page 27 – or compose your own. Play the bass-line and chord pattern on suitable instruments.

2 Add a simple melody above your pattern.

3 Compose or improvise two or more variations on your pattern.

4 Make a recording of your piece. Then listen to it, and discuss it.

In this ceiling painting, Renaissance musicians are playing (clockwise, from the left): plucked string instruments, bowed string instruments, cornetts, and sackbuts.

**Fingerprints of
musical style**

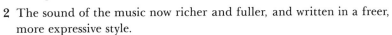

The main characteristics of Renaissance music (*c.*1450–1600)

1 Music still based on the Medieval church modes, but these now treated with greater freedom.

2 The sound of the music now richer and fuller, and written in a freer, more expressive style.

3 Composers aim to blend together the strands in the musical texture, rather than contrast them one against another.

4 A greater awareness of harmony, the flow and progression of chords; a smoother treatment of discords.

5 The music may be in simple chordal style (homophonic texture); or in contrapuntal style (polyphonic texture), using imitation to weave together the musical strands to create a continuously flowing, seamless texture.

6 Church music: most typical forms – the Mass, motet, and anthem; some pieces intended to be sung *a cappella*, mainly contrapuntal with much imitation; other church music accompanied by instruments, e.g. pieces in polychoral style making use of antiphony, and often involving strong musical contrasts between the groups.

7 Secular (non-sacred) music: a rich variety of songs (e.g. madrigal, ballett, ayre, chanson) often making use of the technique known as word-painting; dances (e.g. pavan and galliard, passamezzo, basse danse), and also instrumental pieces (e.g. fantasia, variations, canzona).

8 The characteristic timbres of Renaissance instruments, many forming families – the same instruments in different sizes and pitches (e.g. viols, recorders, shawms, crumhorns).

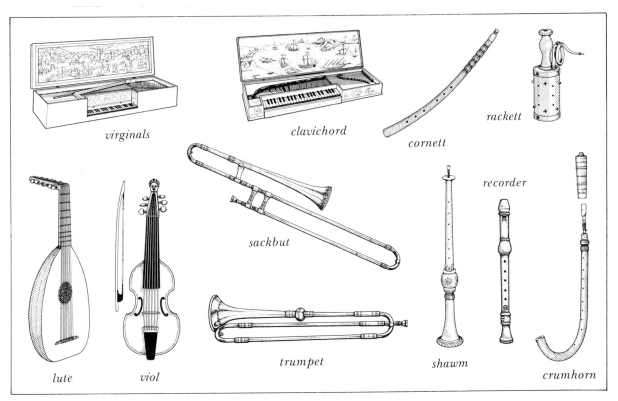

virginals

clavichord

cornett

rackett

recorder

sackbut

lute

viol

trumpet

shawm

crumhorn

Making musical connections

Each of the three Renaissance instrumental pieces on pages 27 and 28 is structured on a repeating bass-line and its chord pattern. Listen to a rather different piece which is also structured on a repeating chord pattern: *West End Blues*, recorded by **Louis Armstrong and his Hot Five** in 1929. This is a typical 12-bar blues, based on this pattern of chords lasting 12 bars (three lines, of four bars each):

bar:	①	②	③	④
chords: $\frac{4}{4}$	/ / / /	/ / / /	/ / / /	/ / / /
	Eb(I)	Eb	Eb	Eb^7

	⑤	⑥	⑦	⑧
	/ / / /	/ / / /	/ / / /	/ / / /
	Ab(IV)	Ab^7	Eb	Eb

	⑨	⑩	⑪	⑫
	/ / / /	/ / / /	/ / / /	/ / / /
	Bb^7(V^7)	Bb^7	Eb	Eb (Bb^7)

Throughout the blues, this chord pattern is repeated. Each playing of the chord pattern is called a **chorus**. A chorus may feature improvisation by one or more soloists, or it may be played by all members of the ensemble, improvising together.

trumpet

West End Blues begins with an introduction – an unaccompanied trumpet solo brilliantly improvised by Louis Armstrong – and then there are five choruses. This plan shows how the piece is structured:

Introduction:	solo – trumpet improvisation (Armstrong), unaccompanied
12-bar chorus: 1	ensemble – in collective improvisation, with Armstrong leading
2	solo – accompanied by ensemble
3	duet – instrumental and vocal (Armstrong 'scat-singing' – singing nonsense syllables)
4	solo – piano improvisation (Earl Hines), unaccompanied
5	mainly ensemble in collective improvisation
Coda:	ensemble – slow, sustained chords

The succession of choruses forms a set of improvised variations on a theme and its chord pattern (chorus 1 is already a variation on the melody of the original song 'West End Blues').

In some choruses, certain chords in the basic pattern are varied – particularly in one chorus, as the improvisation 'takes flight'.

Assignment 23

🔾🔾 **39**

1 Play, or listen as your teacher plays, the basic chord pattern on which *West End Blues* is based.

2 Listen to the recording of *West End Blues*, following the plan of the piece outlined in the box above.

Assignment 24   Listen to *West End Blues* two or three times more.

1 (a) In chorus 2, which instrument plays solo?

(b) In chorus 3, which instrument duets with Armstrong's voice?

(c) Chorus 5 is mainly for the full ensemble – but which instruments are 'spotlighted' towards the end?

2 (a) In which chorus of this blues does the music venture furthest away from the basic chord pattern (as shown opposite)?

(b) Describe the mood and the expressive qualities of the Introduction. Then choose one of the 12-bar choruses and do the same.

Assignment 25   Try your own performance of this blues, called ***Long Handled Shovel***:

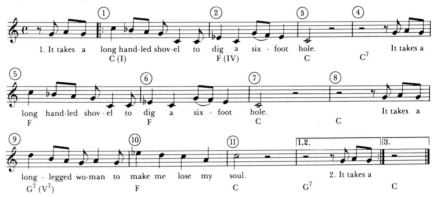

2. It takes a big-hearted woman to make a man feel glad.
   It takes a big-hearted woman to make a man feel glad.
   But then a short-tempered woman will make a man feel bad.

3. I got a two-timin' woman, and she's the worst aroun'.
   I got a two-timin' woman, and she's the worst aroun'.
   I'm gonna grab me a train, gonna get out of this town.

1 Form a group. Some of you sing or play the melody. Others accompany on a mixture of instruments, playing a steady four beats of the chord in each bar (see page 13 for the notes of the chords in this blues pattern). Performers on melody instruments could take turns to improvise short 'breaks' in response to the phrases of the blues melody (at bars 3/4, 7/8, 11/12). Those playing or singing the melody could perform it as written – or perhaps in a rhythmically freer version. Suggestion:

(etc.)

2 When you know this blues well, compose/improvise two variations on the melody and its 12-bar chord pattern – with new, responding 'breaks' at the ends of the phrases. Then record a complete performance:

1	verse 1 – voice(s) and instruments
2	first variation on melody and basic chord pattern
3	verse 2 – voice(s) and instruments
4	second variation on melody and basic chord pattern
5	verse 3 – voice(s) and instruments

One popular type of piece for instruments in the 16th century was the *canzona*. Italian composers often wrote canzonas in the same style as polychoral church music – using two or more groups of instruments, spaced apart to emphasize effects of antiphony and contrasts of various kinds.

QO 40   Listen to Giovanni Gabrieli's **Canzona XIV** (1597) for three instrumental groups. Here are some points to listen for:

> • the use of physical space for musical effect
> • sometimes one group only, sometimes two, sometimes all three
> • antiphonal effects between the various groups
> • sometimes the effect of challenge, or opposition, between groups
> • contrasts – e.g. in timbres, pitches, dynamics, textures
> • overlapping or interweaving of musical ideas between groups

Assignment 26   Investigate excerpts from two 20th-century compositions which also exploit physical space, and contrast various instrumental groups of ensembles.

QO 41 A   1 Stockhausen: **Gruppen**, meaning 'groups'. (See also page 80.) Listen to the third quarter or so of this 24-minute piece. The music is for 109 performers playing woodwinds, brass, percussion (including keyed glockenspiel, marimba, vibraphone, celesta, and xylorimba), 2 harps, piano, electric guitar, and strings. Stockhausen groups these into three equal orchestras, widely separated and surrounding the audience on three sides (see the photograph, opposite). During this extract, listen for:

• the use of physical space – antiphony between the three orchestras;
• contrasts of timbres, dynamics; changing speeds and textures;
• later: low brass, *staccato* – then antiphony between brass groups, muted (distant) and unmuted;
• sustained brass chords, swinging from group to group;
• a passage featuring piano;
• percussion (skin and metal) of all three orchestras;
• brass joins in; music builds to a *fortissimo* dense climax . . .

QO 41 B   2 Harrison Birtwistle: **Verses for Ensembles**. Listen to the first ten minutes or so of this piece. The separate groups of instruments here consist of a brass quintet, two woodwind quintets (one higher in pitch than the other), and two percussion ensembles (one of pitched instruments – xylophones and glockenspiels – and the other of a variety of unpitched instruments). The five groups are spacially separated, and the layout is specified in the score. In the case of the woodwind and percussion, the same performers play in both their groups – moving, according to which instrument they are to play next. Players also move for solo passages.

During this music, besides many kinds of contrast in *sound*, notice also the effect of contrast between sound and *silence*.

Assignment 27   1 Listen again to the music by Gabrieli, Stockhausen, and Birtwistle. Are any of the characteristics of Gabrieli's piece (listed in the box above) apparent in the 20th-century pieces also?
    2 Afterwards, try the composing and performing assignment (56) on page 34 of *New Assignments and Practice Scores*.

A favourite technique of Renaissance composers, in vocal music, was that of *word-painting* – vivid musical illustrations to bring out the special meaning of certain words. The effect may be heard in the instrumental accompaniment as well as (or instead of) the vocal part in the music.

Investigate the effect of word-painting in a 20th-century piece: part of the song **'The Merry Cuckoo'** from Benjamin Britten's **Spring Symphony**. Britten scores the Symphony for solo voices, boys' choir, mixed choir, and orchestra; but this particular song is for four performers only: tenor voice, and three trumpets.

> The merry cuckoo, messenger of Spring,
> His trumpet shrill hath thrice already sounded,
> That warns all lovers wait upon their king,
> Who now is coming forth with garlands crowned.
> With noise whereof the choir of birds resounded,
> Their anthems sweet devised of love's praise,
> That all the woods their echoes back rebounded,
> As if they knew the meaning of their lays . . .

Assignment 28

1 Read through the words. (Can you spot any which you would *expect* Britten to select for word-painting?)

▢▢ 42

2 Follow the words as you listen to the music. Which ideas does Britten 'paint'? How are they illustrated, or expressed, in the music?

Assignment 29

▢▢ 43

Listen again to the Renaissance dance, *Passamezzo* (page 27). Then listen to a folk-dance from Yugoslavia, called **Kolo Round**. It is played by an ensemble made up of: fiddle, *jedinka* (fipple flute), *tamburica* (lute-like plucked string instrument), accordion, and string bass.

As you listen to each dance, match one item from each category:

Instruments	Rhythm	Bass-line	Harmony	Texture	Tonality
similar in type	simple	8 bars, repeating	based on four chords	changes	major
	complex			remains the same	minor
mixture of types		mainly 2-note *ostinato*	mainly one chord, repeated		

A rehearsal of Stockhausen's Gruppen, *conducted by Stockhausen (orchestra 1, left), Bruno Maderna (orchestra 2, centre), and Pierre Boulez (orchestra 3, right)*

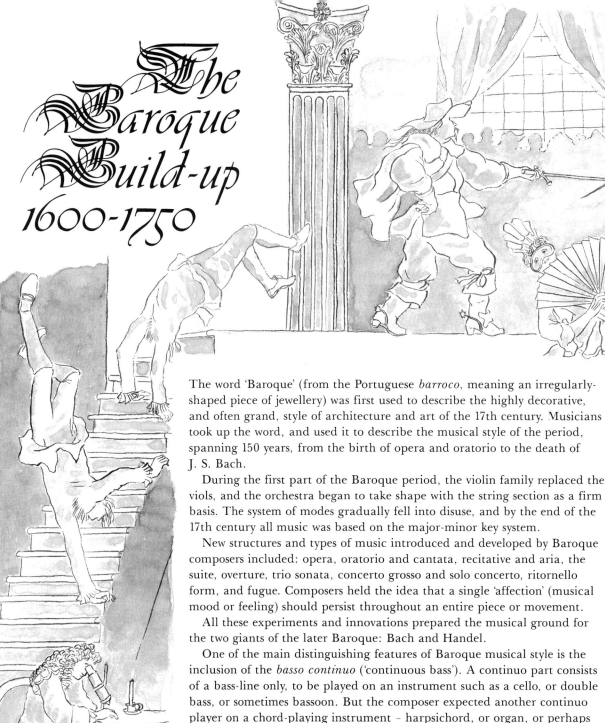

The Baroque Build-up 1600-1750

The word 'Baroque' (from the Portuguese *barroco*, meaning an irregularly-shaped piece of jewellery) was first used to describe the highly decorative, and often grand, style of architecture and art of the 17th century. Musicians took up the word, and used it to describe the musical style of the period, spanning 150 years, from the birth of opera and oratorio to the death of J. S. Bach.

During the first part of the Baroque period, the violin family replaced the viols, and the orchestra began to take shape with the string section as a firm basis. The system of modes gradually fell into disuse, and by the end of the 17th century all music was based on the major-minor key system.

New structures and types of music introduced and developed by Baroque composers included: opera, oratorio and cantata, recitative and aria, the suite, overture, trio sonata, concerto grosso and solo concerto, ritornello form, and fugue. Composers held the idea that a single 'affection' (musical mood or feeling) should persist throughout an entire piece or movement.

All these experiments and innovations prepared the musical ground for the two giants of the later Baroque: Bach and Handel.

One of the main distinguishing features of Baroque musical style is the inclusion of the *basso continuo* ('continuous bass'). A continuo part consists of a bass-line only, to be played on an instrument such as a cello, or double bass, or sometimes bassoon. But the composer expected another continuo player on a chord-playing instrument - harpsichord, or organ, or perhaps lute - to use skill and musicianship to improvise chords upon the bass-line, filling in the harmonies, and also decorating the musical texture. The notes of the basso continuo provided clues to the necessary harmonies, but composers often wrote figures below the notes, clearly indicating the chords which were expected - and so such a bass-line is called a 'figured bass'. The idea of an accompaniment played by continuo instruments was to persist throughout the Baroque, and provide the basis for the harmonies, and the texture, of almost every type of piece.

Timechart: Baroque composers

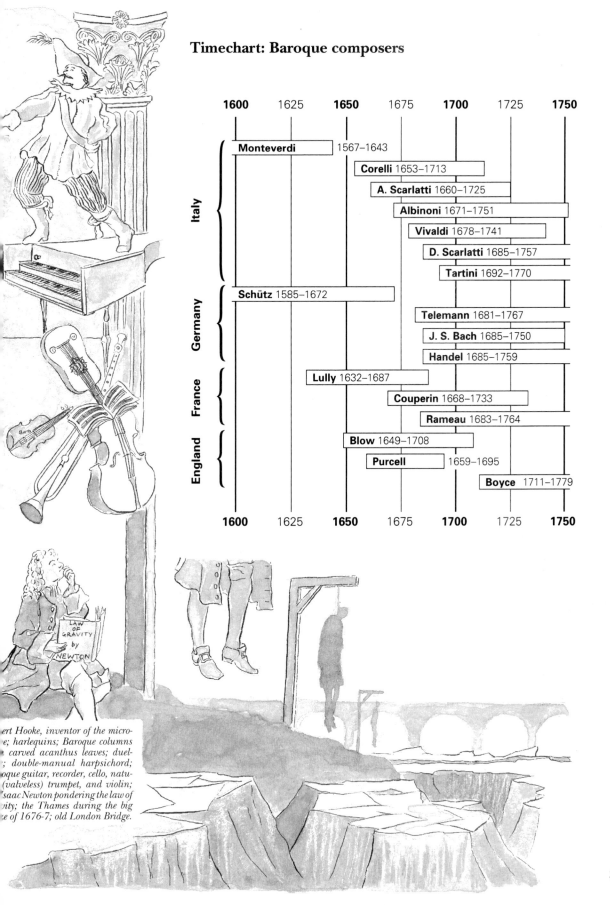

	1600	1625	1650	1675	1700	1725	1750

Italy

- Monteverdi 1567–1643
- Corelli 1653–1713
- A. Scarlatti 1660–1725
- Albinoni 1671–1751
- Vivaldi 1678–1741
- D. Scarlatti 1685–1757
- Tartini 1692–1770

Germany

- Schütz 1585–1672
- Telemann 1681–1767
- J. S. Bach 1685–1750
- Handel 1685–1759

France

- Lully 1632–1687
- Couperin 1668–1733
- Rameau 1683–1764

England

- Blow 1649–1708
- Purcell 1659–1695
- Boyce 1711–1779

	1600	1625	1650	1675	1700	1725	1750

*...ert Hooke, inventor of the micro-
...e; harlequins; Baroque columns
... carved acanthus leaves; duel-
...; double-manual harpsichord;
...oque guitar, recorder, cello, natu-
...(valveless) trumpet, and violin;
...saac Newton pondering the law of
...vity; the Thames during the big
...e of 1676-7; old London Bridge.*

LAW OF GRAVITY by NEWTON

Baroque music for orchestra

It was during the Baroque period that the orchestra first began to take shape. Here are some typical features of the Baroque orchestra:

- a firm basis of strings – to which composers would add other instruments as occasion offered: one or two flutes (or recorders), oboes, bassoons, perhaps horns, occasionally trumpets and kettle drums;
- the ever-present sound of organ or harpsichord **continuo** – the player continuing, throughout the music, to build up chords on the bass-line, filling out the harmonies and decorating the textures;
- effects of **contrast**, especially of dynamics and of timbres – often, bright 'ribbons' of sound, such as oboes or trumpets, against a background of strings and continuo; or contrasting 'blocks' of sound of different timbres – for instance, strings and wind alternately, then *tutti* (everyone together).

⊙⊙ 44 Listen to the two **Bourrées** from Bach's **Orchestral Suite No. 4 in D major**. A **suite** is a set of pieces, often dances, grouped together to form a complete work. Below, you can see the kind of orchestra Bach uses for this Suite. The Bourrées are played alternately, in 'sandwich' fashion:

Bourrée I	Bourrée II	Bourrée I

Together, they make up a piece in what is called 'minuet and trio' form – with Bourrée II acting as the 'trio'.

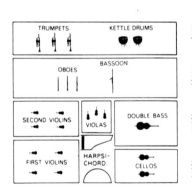

Bourrée I

harpsichord

Bourrée II

[*Bourrée I* again, without repeats]

36

Assignment 30

Listen again to this pair of dances by Bach.

(a) Bourrée I begins with a bright 'ribbon' of trumpet sound. In which bars do you next hear this same effect?

(b) In what other way does Bach contrast timbres in Bourrée I?

(c) In Bourrée II, which of these plays a 'running' accompaniment?

double bass	bassoon	trumpet	harpsichord

(d) Mention another way in which Bourrée II contrasts with Bourrée I.

(e) In a Baroque piece or movement, the same *mood* is usually kept from beginning to end. Describe the mood of these two Bourrées.

One of the most important instrumental forms used by Baroque composers was the **concerto**. There were two main types, each based upon the idea of contrast:

• the **concerto grosso** – contrasting a small group of solo instruments, called the *concertino* (meaning 'little ensemble'), against a string orchestra, called either the *ripieno* ('filling'), *concerto grosso* ('big ensemble'), or *tutti* ('all', 'everyone');

• the **solo concerto** – featuring a single soloist (often given some difficult and exciting passages to play) pitted against the weight of a string orchestra.

The concerto grosso grew from the ideas of opposition and contrast found in pieces in polychoral style, for two or more groups of musicians, by composers such as Giovanni Gabrieli. In the solo concerto – one against many – the idea of contrast became stronger still.

In both these types of concerto, quicker movements (and sometimes slower movements also) were built up in **ritornello form**. The music starts off with the *ritornello* (meaning 'little return') played by the ripieno group, usually with the soloist(s) joining in. This is the main theme, and it returns at various points throughout the movement. It may reappear in full, or it may be altered or shortened. The first and last times that it is heard, it is in the tonic (the 'home' key). Other appearances are usually in contrasting keys.

Between appearances of the ritornello there are contrasting sections of music called *episodes*. These feature the soloist (or solo group).

Ritornello	Episode 1	Ritornello	Episode 2	Ritornello	
tutti	soloist(s)	tutti	soloist(s)	tutti	(and so on)

Listen to the final movement of Handel's **Concerto Grosso, Opus 3 No. 1**. First, investigate the melody-line score of this movement printed on the next page. Handel uses an orchestra made up of: 2 oboes, 2 bassoons, string orchestra, and harpsichord continuo.

45   Listen to the music, following the score.

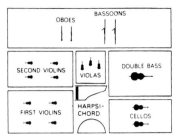

'Hommage à J.S. Bach' by the French painter Georges Braque

Assignment 31

1 Listen again to this movement built up in ritornello form (this time, *not* following the score). As you listen, complete this chart; mention the solo instrument(s) featured in each episode of the ritornello structure.

Ritornello	tutti
Episode 1	featuring . . . . .
Ritornello	

2 Listen again – either following the score or the chart you made of the structure of the music. This time, pick out the sounds of the harpsichord continuo. In which bars, or in which section of the music, do you notice the continuo player particularly decorating the texture of the music?

Fugue

At the beginning of the Baroque period, the main style of musical texture was *homophonic* – melody supported by simple chords. But before long, there was a return to *contrapuntal* (or *polyphonic*) texture – two or more equally important melodic lines weaving along in counterpoint.

One of the most important types of contrapuntal piece is the **fugue**. It is essentially based on the musical device called *imitation*. A fugue is usually written in three or four parts called 'voices' (whether, in fact, the

39

fugue is vocal or instrumental). The detailed structure of a fugue can be rather complex, but the main points are these:

- the entire piece usually grows from a single tune, called the **subject**;
- the subject is first given out in one voice only;
- then it is imitated by the other voices in turn, each at its appropriate pitch;
- during the fugue, the subject reappears in contrasting keys – now in one voice, now in another – but to end the fugue, it is heard at least once in the tonic key.

A lively example is **Fugue No. 9 in D minor** from Bach's *The Art of Fugue* – a collection of fugues and four canons based on this main theme:

Fugue No. 9 has its own distinctive *subject*:

But before long, the main theme enters and is heard in long notes, weaving along in counterpoint with the fugue subject:

46 Assignment 32   In the recording on the cassette, Fugue No. 9 is played by harpsichord and solo strings. During the performance, listen especially for appearances of the fugue subject – and also, for entries of the main theme in long notes.

47 Assignment 33   1 Listen to a rather different-sounding performance of **Fugue No. 9 in D minor** – by the **Swingle Singers**.
2 Compare both performances of Bach's fugue. Mention any differences – or similarities – that you notice.
3 Which performance do you prefer? Give reasons for your choice.

Assignment 34   If possible, try your own group performance of part (or all) of Ernst Toch's 'Geographical Fugue'* from *Gesprochene Musik*. This is for speaking (not singing) chorus, and is based on the rhythms of place names, such as Trinidad, the Mississippi, Honolulu, the Popacatepetl, Canada, Mexico, Tibet. A performance needs concentration – but can be great fun!

* Available from The Cambridge Music Shop, All Saints' Passage, Cambridge

Music on a ground bass	This was a special way of structuring variations, popular with composers of the 16th and 17th centuries.

- the theme – or **ground** – is repeated again and again in the bass;
- the ground may be only a few notes long, or it may be a complete melody;
- above the repeating ground, the composer weaves a continuous, varying texture of melody and harmonies;
- sometimes, the phrasing of the melody overlaps the joins between repetitions of the ground – binding the texture closely together and giving the music a more continuous flow;
- a ground bass is sometimes called a *basso ostinato* ('obstinately repeating bass-line').

The ground bass was especially popular with the English composer, Henry Purcell. The music below is Dido's song 'Ah! Belinda' from his opera ***Dido and Aeneas***, composed in 1689.

Assignment 35
1 Before listening, investigate the score of the music.
    (a) How many bars long is the ground on which Purcell structures this song?
    (b) Does the ground always appear at the same pitch (in the same key)?

2 As you listen, notice where the melody sometimes overlaps the last bar of one playing of the ground and the first bar of the next.
    As the printed music ends, Dido sings her last note (bar 56) and there is an instrumental *coda* to round off the song. On the last note of the final playing of the ground, Belinda joins in: 'Grief increases by concealing . . .'

48

Assignment 36
    (a) How many times is the ground played during the coda?

    (b) How are the instrumental sounds of the coda different from the sounds which have accompanied Dido's singing?

    (c) If you can, listen to Dido's other famous song, the lament 'When I am laid in earth'* and compare it with 'Ah! Belinda'. What features do these two songs have in common? How are they different?

[* recorded on *Form and Design* cassette 2]

Fingerprints of musical style

The main characteristics of Baroque music (1600–1750)

1 Early Baroque composers favour a light, homophonic musical texture – melody plus simple chordal accompaniment; but before long, there is a return to polyphonic (contrapuntal) textures.

2 The basso continuo, or figured bass, becomes the musical foundation for most types of piece – providing a purposeful bass-line (sometimes, a 'walking bass') making the music move steadily onwards.

3 The same musical mood is usually kept throughout an entire piece.

4 The violin family takes over from the viols; the orchestra begins to take shape, with the string section as a firm basis – always with keyboard continuo (harpsichord or organ) filling out the harmonies above the figured bass and decorating the musical texture.

5 The system of modes falls out of use by the end of the 17th century; music is now based on major and minor scales.

6 Typical forms used by Baroque composers: binary, ternary (including the *da capo* aria), rondeau, variations (including the ground bass, chaconne, passacaglia), ritornello form, fugue.

7 Main types of Baroque music:
vocal – chorale, recitative and aria, opera, oratorio, cantata;
instrumental – Italian overture, French overture, toccata, prelude, chorale prelude, dance suite, trio sonatas (sonata da camera, sonata da chiesa), concerto grosso, solo concerto.

8 Often, energetic rhythms drive the music forward; melodies are frequently long and flowing, and decorated with ornaments (e.g. appoggiaturas, trills); contrasts (particularly in concertos) of instrumental timbres, of few instruments against many, of loud contrasted against soft ('terraced dynamics', sometimes echo effects), and of 'blocks' of sound of different timbres (e.g. strings and wind alternately, then together).

Making musical connections

The music of Purcell's song 'Ah! Belinda' (page 41) is structured on a ground bass, or *basso ostinato*. Here is another piece – very different in sound and style, but built up in a similar way: **'Child in Time'** by the rock group **Deep Purple**. For much of the piece, the music is structured on this ground, or ostinato, heard in the bass:

$$\|\colon \quad G \; G \mid A \qquad G \; G \mid A \qquad F \; F \mid G \quad G \; G \mid A \quad \colon\|$$

The piece is built up in eight sections. Here is a plan showing the first five sections, with approximate elapsed timing, and indicating some of the main musical events.

0′00″   0′49″   1′53″

1	2	3

Introduction, setting mood
 	
keyboards, percussion
	words sung through, complete
	
	keyboards join in ostinato
		mainly vocalized
		
		           more excited,
		                frantic . . .

ostinato [3 times] / / /	continues [4 times] / / / /	continues [6 times] / / / / / /

3′24″   3′38″   7′25″

4	5		6
bolero rhythm, *ff*!	keyboards featured	guitar solo increasing build-up, frenzy . . .	
?	?		

Section 7 begins at 8′14″, section 8 begins at 9′15″, and the piece ends at around 12′04″ (version as recorded on: double album, *Made in Japan*; or mid-price compilation album, *24 Carat Purple*).

Assignment 37

Listen to 'Child in Time' following the plan above – and listening on when the plan ends. During the Introduction, notice especially the timbre and texture of the music, and the repeating ground or ostinato.

(a) In which section does the ostinato stop? And in which section does it set off again?

(b) Section 7 is similar to one of the previous sections. Which one?

Assignment 38

1 Listen again to 'Child in Time'.
   (a) How is excitement and tension built up during section 3?
   (b) Which section, do you think, contains the most *improvisation*?
   (c) In which section does the biggest climax occur? How is the tension built up? How is it released?
   (d) Comment on the different uses of the *voice* in this song.

2 Make your own plan of sections 6, 7, and 8, noting down the most important features of the music. (You may need quite a bit of space for section 8.)

Assignment 39

Form a group of musicians, and compose your own piece structured on a ground, or ostinato.
1 Decide whether your ostinato is to have rhythm (as Deep Purple's), or to be mainly in notes of equal value (as Purcell's).
2 Above your repeating ostinato, add a rhythmic part on one or more percussion instruments – matching the mood of your ostinato.
3 Compose/improvise a melodic line above your ostinato – or a texture of melody and harmonies.
4 Perhaps you could make up some words to fit your melodic line.
5 Decide whether your music should keep to the same mood throughout – or change mood, and perhaps also build up to a climax.
6 Also decide whether your ostinato continues right through – or stops, perhaps dramatically, at some point and then starts up again.

A strong feature of many pieces of the Baroque period is what is called a **walking bass** – a purposeful bass-line, making the music move steadily onwards. It is often in notes of equal value (e.g. crotchets, or quavers).

Assignment 40

1 Listen again to Bourrée I from Bach's Orchestral Suite No. 4 in D, concentrating on the bass-line. Here, it moves mainly in crotchets – but the pace is quite lively (perhaps 'jogging' rather than 'walking'!).

(etc.)

   (a) What kind of *range* does this bass-line have – wide, medium, or narrow?
   (b) In which bar or bars of the printed music does the widest leap occur?

49 2 Contrast this Baroque walking bass with a typical *reggae* bass-line, such as that of '**Lively Up Yourself**' by **Bob Marley and the Wailers** (on their album *Natty Dread*).
   (a) What main differences do you hear between the reggae bass-line and the walking bass?
   (b) How many beats to a bar are there in 'Lively Up Yourself'?
   (c) Name the instrument which plays this reggae bass-line. Which other instruments play the backing in this song?

Assignment 41

1 Listen again to Bach's Fugue No. 9 in D minor (page 40), in either version. The style of the musical texture is *contrapuntal* – the weaving together of two or more melodic lines (in this piece, most often four). Each time the main theme appears, the fugue subject is always heard weaving along at the same time. Spot when the main theme is heard *above* the fugue subject – and when it is heard *below* it.

2 Contrast the contrapuntal texture of Bach's fugue with a piece in *monophonic* texture – a single melodic line, with no supporting harmonies. **Kalenda Maya** is a colourful dance-song by the 12th-century Provençal troubadour, Raimbaut de Vaqueiras. His poem begins: 'The first of May, but neither leaf nor flower nor birdsong can give me joy till I receive a message from my love . . .'

   The words are vigorously sung in what the singer believes would have been the style of Raimbaut's time (you may find the sound rather startling!). Here is the complete music of this dance-song – three phrases, each heard many times over:

 50

(a) What instrument plays the melody throughout this dance-song?
(b) Besides drums playing a vivid rhythmic accompaniment, a rebec – a bowed instrument with three strings – also takes part. Does it provide:
   an ostinato; a drone; or a walking bass?
(c) What do you like or dislike about this music?

rebec

Medieval peasants performing a round-dance to celebrate the first of May

Assignment 42   In 1938, Stravinsky composed a Concerto in E flat which he entitled *Dumbarton Oaks*. It is for a small orchestra of fifteen instruments:

flute	2 horns	3 violins
clarinet		3 violas
bassoon		2 cellos
		2 double basses

Stravinsky deliberately modelled *Dumbarton Oaks* on the style of the *concerto grosso* of the time of Handel and Bach (in particular, Bach's Brandenburg Concertos). Passages for everyone playing together (*tutti*) are contrasted against passages spotlighting various members of the orchestra as soloists – either singly, or in small groups.

The last movement of *Dumbarton Oaks* is built up in ritornello form (see page 37). The recurring *ritornello* is based on this crisp, rhythmic idea:

In the opening ritornello, this idea appears three times.

⬭⬭ 51   Follow this basic plan of the music as you listen:

Ritornello (0′00″)	tutti (the full orchestra)
Episode 1 (0′43″)	an idea (including *x* from the ritornello) first played by the horns; then in turn by flute, bassoon, horn 2; later, by basses with horns and bassoon, and then violins and violas in octaves (this episode ends with scurrying violins)
Ritornello (1′57″)	tutti
Episode 2 (2′13″)	featuring two solo violins (above an *ostinato* on flute and clarinet); then solo flute and clarinet; and then the two violins again, joined by two cellos
Ritornello (3′12″)	rather brief: strings alternating with wind
Episode 3 (3′20″)	first, full orchestra; later, solos for clarinet, violin, horn 1, flute
Ritornello (4′03″)	beginning on strings against a busy *ostinato* on clarinet and bassoon; the music gradually builds up until the end.

Listen again to the movement from the concerto grosso by Handel (page 38) and to this movement from *Dumbarton Oaks* by Stravinsky. Mention the main differences – and also any similarities – that you notice between these two pieces. For instance, consider:

harmony;   rhythm;   timbres;   contrasts;   form/structure.

The Classical Ideal 1750-1810

The word 'classical' is sometimes used, in a rather loose way, when people think of music as being divided into two very broad categories: 'classical' music and 'popular' music. Musicians, however, use the word 'Classical' (with a capital 'C') with a special, very much more precise meaning – referring specifically to music composed between 1750 and about 1810. This rather brief period in musical history includes the music of Haydn and Mozart, and the earlier works of Beethoven.

During the Classical period, the Baroque trio sonata gave way to the Classical sonata, and the Italian overture grew into the Classical symphony. The orchestra, which had started to take shape during the Baroque period, now began to grow and become more balanced, and eventually the harpsichord continuo fell out of use.

Important features of Classical musical style are: grace and beauty of line (melody), perfection of form and design (the shape and structure of the music), clarity and simplicity, proportion and balance, moderation and control. In particular, the Classical composer aims to strike the ideal balance between expressiveness and formal structure. Whereas in a Baroque piece or movement the composer keeps the same mood throughout, a Classical composer uses a richer variety of contrasting tunes, rhythms, keys, dynamics (now making use of *crescendo*, *diminuendo*, *sforzando*), with frequent changes of timbre, and also of mood. Although counterpoint is not forgotten, the texture of the music is more likely to be basically homophonic – melody supported by chordal accompaniment.

The main types of vocal music composed during the Classical period were the Mass, and opera (many fine examples by Mozart). But it was instrumental music which was predominant, the main types being the sonata, symphony, concerto, trio, string quartet, and 'entertainment' works such as the divertimento and the serenade. All these usually had at least one of their movements structured in the most important musical form of the Classical period: sonata form (described on page 55).

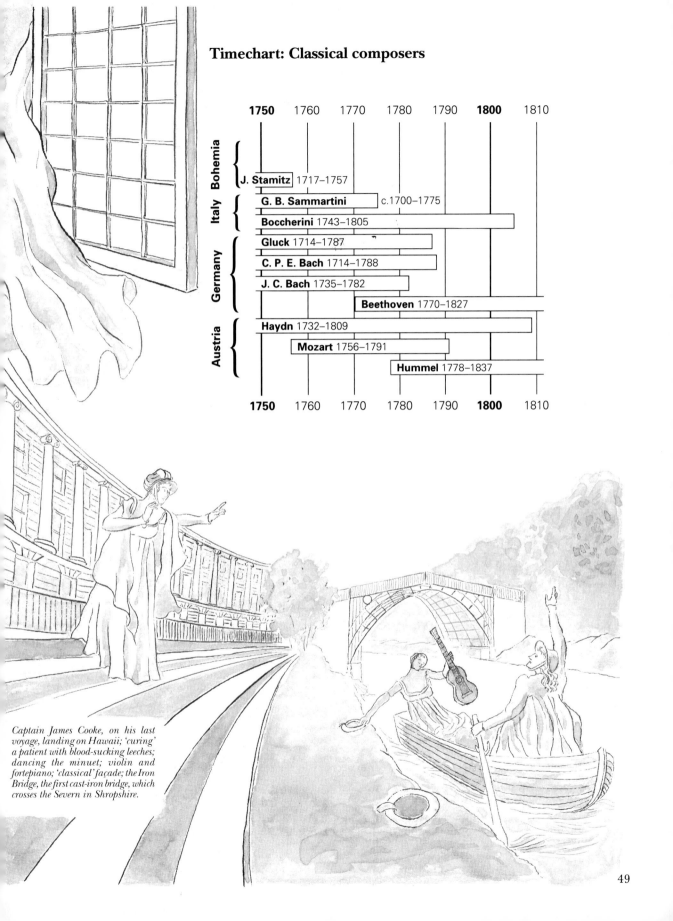

Timechart: Classical composers

	1750	1760	1770	1780	1790	1800	1810

Bohemia
J. Stamitz 1717–1757

Italy
G. B. Sammartini c.1700–1775
Boccherini 1743–1805

Germany
Gluck 1714–1787
C. P. E. Bach 1714–1788
J. C. Bach 1735–1782
Beethoven 1770–1827

Austria
Haydn 1732–1809
Mozart 1756–1791
Hummel 1778–1837

	1750	1760	1770	1780	1790	1800	1810

Captain James Cooke, on his last voyage, landing on Hawaii; 'curing' a patient with blood-sucking leeches; dancing the minuet; violin and fortepiano; 'classical' façade; the Iron Bridge, the first cast-iron bridge, which crosses the Severn in Shropshire.

49

Sonata structures

Of the larger musical forms and structures used by Classical composers, the **sonata** was the most important. The Classical sonata was a work in several movements, for one or two instruments only – for instance, piano; or violin and piano. If the composer chose to write for three instruments, the work was then called a *trio*; if four, a *quartet*. A **symphony** is in fact a sonata for orchestra. And a **concerto** is a sonata for one or more solo instruments with orchestra.

Symphonies and works such as trios and quartets were structured in four movements, contrasted in speed and character, and usually set out as shown in the plan below. A sonata might be in four, sometimes three, movements. The Classical concerto did not include the minuet, and so was always in three movements.

> • First movement – at a fairly fast speed; usually built up in what is called **sonata form**.
> • Second movement – at a slower speed, and more song-like; often in ternary form, or variations, or perhaps sonata form again.
> • Third movement – at this point, Haydn and Mozart wrote a minuet and trio; Beethoven later transformed this into the much brisker and more vigorous *scherzo* (meaning 'a joke').
> • Fourth movement (Finale) – at a swift speed, often light-hearted in mood; in rondo form, or sonata form, or perhaps in a mixture of both (sonata-rondo form); sometimes, variations.

clarinet

As an example of characteristic music of the Classical period, investigate the slow second movement of the **Clarinet Concerto in A major** by Mozart. Mozart builds up this movement in ternary form (A^1 B A^2), with a *link* and a short solo *cadenza* joining B and A^2, and a *coda* to round off:

A^1	B	Link, plus cadenza	A^2	Coda
statement	contrast (an episode)		restatement	(rounding off)

52 Assignment 43

1 Listen to the opening section (A^1) of the movement, following the music printed at the top of the opposite page.
 (a) Which of these tempo markings matches this music?
  adagio; *allegro*; *vivace*.
 (b) Which two of these words describe the style of the accompaniment?
  jerky; wavy; *staccato*; *legato*; syncopated.
 (c) Which of the following is a feature of bars 17–20 and 25–28?

  | pedal | imitation | pizzicato | inversion |

2 Listen again to this first section of the movement. How does Mozart achieve shape and balance in the music – from the point of view of timbre, texture, structure/phrasing?

53 Now listen to section B of the music (printed below), followed by the *link* passage.

Assignment 44 Listen again, discovering answers to these questions:
1 How is the accompaniment in section B different from that in section A?
2 Compared with section A, how is the music for the solo clarinet different in section B?
3 During the *link* passage, how does Mozart give the music a sense of greater urgency?

54 **Assignment 45** Now listen to the rest of the music – picking up with the link passage. In this slow movement, the passage for the solo (unaccompanied) clarinet called a *cadenza* is short and simple.
1 When music A returns as A^2, is it exactly the same as it was at first, or does Mozart make any changes?
2 In the *coda* which rounds off the movement, is the music for the solo clarinet most like music A, or music B?

Chamber music

This is music written for a small group of solo musicians, and intended to be played in a room (chamber), rather than in a large hall. The most popular of all types of chamber work is the string quartet. This is really a *sonata* for four string instruments: two violins, viola, and cello - and it is usually in four movements (see page 50).

The composer most responsible for shaping and perfecting the string quartet was Haydn (he composed at least 68). Listen to the third movement of his **String Quartet in B♭, Opus 50 No. 1**. The music is structured in minuet and trio form:

A^1: Minuet	B: Trio	A^2: Minuet again
	(a contrast)	(without repeats)

1st Violin   2nd Violin

Viola   Cello

52

Da capo al Fine

Assignment 46

(a) The Minuet section is structured in binary form, and it is based on a single tune. How many bars long is this tune?

(b) How many times is the tune heard during the Minuet? Name the instruments which play it, in turn.

(c) How does the beginning of the Trio provide a contrast to the Minuet?

(d) Describe two ways in which Haydn makes use of the rhythmic effect of *syncopation* during the Trio.

(e) In which of these musical forms is the Trio structured?

| binary form | ternary form |

Give a reason for your choice.

The Classical orchestra

The orchestra, which had started to take shape during the Baroque period, began to grow and become more balanced during the Classical period. By the end of the 18th century, the four main woodwinds were combined in pairs to form a self-contained woodwind section. Horns were always included, and often trumpets and drums. For a time, this orchestra was accepted as standard:

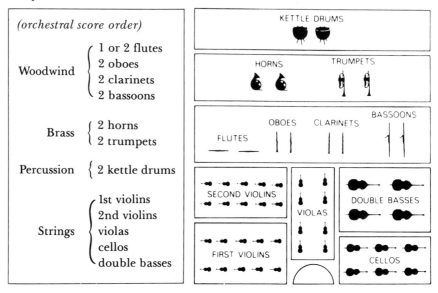

(orchestral score order)

Woodwind	{	1 or 2 flutes 2 oboes 2 clarinets 2 bassoons
Brass	{	2 horns 2 trumpets
Percussion	{	2 kettle drums
Strings	{	1st violins 2nd violins violas cellos double basses

56 Listen to part of the **Overture to *Don Giovanni*** (1787) by Mozart, composed for exactly the orchestra shown above. Listen for these four main themes:

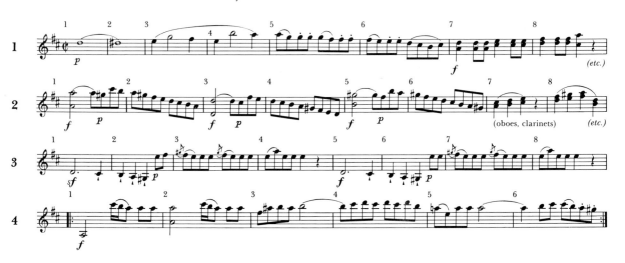

Assignment 47   Listen two or three times more and find answers to these questions, one on each theme:

Theme 1   How is the whole orchestra involved in bars 1–8?

Theme 2   Mention two musical contrasts presented during this theme.

Theme 3   After bar 8, which of the following happens?
  (a) the first two bars are used in imitation;
  (b) Mozart immediately brings in a new tune.

Theme 4   Is this music played by brass and strings, or the full orchestra?

Sonata form   The most important single form or structure used by Classical composers is known as **sonata form**. In most large-scale works, you will find the first movement is built up in this form. It is also sometimes used for other movements, and for single pieces (such as overtures).

A piece or movement in sonata form is structured in three main sections, called *exposition*, *development*, and *recapitulation*. (There may be an introduction before the sonata form really begins.) Here is a basic plan:

Exposition (presentation)			Development (discussion)	Recapitulation (restatement)			Coda
First subject (tonic)	Bridge (changing key)	Second subject (in a new key)	moving through new keys, discussing, developing, combining and opposing ideas from the exposition	First subject (tonic)	Bridge (now altered)	Second subject (*tonic*)	to round off

- **Exposition**   In this section the composer 'exposes', or presents, the material on which the music is to be based. The main ideas are called **subjects** (meaning 'subjects for later discussion'). There are two subjects – and each may consist of a *group* of musical ideas rather than a single melody. The two subjects are contrasted in key, and usually also in mood and character. The **first subject** is presented in the tonic key (the 'home' key). Then follows a **bridge passage** which modulates, and leads to the **second subject** in a new key – often the dominant, or the relative major if the tonic is a minor key. (The exposition may be repeated.)

- **Development**   In this section the composer 'develops' or explores the musical possibilities of any of the ideas presented in the exposition section. A rhythmic or tuneful fragment may be repeated while the music modulates through various keys (but avoiding the tonic key). Fragments of different ideas may be combined, or set into opposition, challenging each other. A strong feeling of tension, of dramatic conflict, may be built up, reaching a climax when the music purposefully makes for 'home' – the tonic key – and the beginning of the recapitulation.

- **Recapitulation**   The composer now 'recapitulates', or restates in a slightly different way, the material of the exposition section. The first subject is heard in the tonic key as before. But the bridge passage is altered so that the second subject *also* now appears in the tonic key.
  The composer then rounds off the movement with a **coda**.

Assignment 48   Listen to part of the first movement of Beethoven's **'Eroica' Symphony** (No. 3 in E♭), composed in 1803 and scored for 'Classical orchestra' plus one extra horn. Beethoven builds up the movement in sonata form. First there is a very brief introduction – two punched chords of E♭ major. Then the exposition begins (see the music on the next page). The **first subject** consists of two main ideas, (a) and (b): (a) begins by outlining the notes of the tonic chord of E♭ major, before slipping down to an unexpected C♯; (b) features the rhythmic device of syncopation (see page 10).

〇〇 | 57   First, listen as far as the end of the bridge passage, following the music printed overleaf.

Is the bridge passage based on a new idea, or an idea already presented?

58 **Assignment 49** The lengthy second subject is structured from a group of six main musical ideas (a) to (f), below. As the music is played, listen for each one.

56

Assignment 50 Now investigate how Beethoven uses some of the ideas from the exposition in the first half of the development section. (The three ideas marked *x*, *y*, and *z* in brackets on the opposite page become very important.) Here are some points to listen for:

- at first the music is shadowy, mysterious, feeling its way . . .
- second subject (a), now with a counterpoint added (listen for rising *staccato* quavers);
- *x* on lower strings, in C minor, then C♯ minor;
- second subject (c) in D minor on violins - combined with *x* in the bass;
- the same soon happens again, beginning in G minor;
- second subject (a) with counterpoint again;
- (music printed below) a *fugato** on second subject (a); then discussion and development of two strongly rhythmic ideas, *z* and *y* - building up drama and tension, and reaching a powerful climax.

Assignment 51

1 In Beethoven's 'Eroica' Symphony, the Classical ideals of grace, simplicity and moderation are strongly challenged - if not overthrown. Beethoven is already forging his powerful personal style which will later influence so many 19th-century Romantic composers. Listen to this third excerpt again, listening especially for these two features in the music:
vigorous syncopations; dramatic dynamic contrasts.

2 In the last part of the excerpt (printed above), how does Beethoven build up drama and tension in the music? How is the tension released?

(* a passage of music similar in style to the beginning of a fugue.)

Fingerprints of musical style

The main characteristics of Classical music (1750–1810)

1 Lighter and clearer in texture, less complicated, than Baroque music; generally tending to be homophonic (melody plus chordal accompaniment) – but counterpoint by no means forgotten.

2 An importance placed upon grace and beauty, proportion and balance, moderation and control; above all: polished and elegant in character with a perfect balance struck between expressiveness and formal structure (the shape, design of the music).

3 Greater variety and contrast of musical materials within a piece: of tunes, keys, rhythms, dynamics – now using *crescendo* (growing gradually louder), *diminuendo* (gradually softer), *sforzando* (forcing the tone, accenting the note or chord); frequent changes of timbre, and mood.

4 The orchestra grows and becomes more balanced, with the woodwind as a self-contained section; the keyboard continuo drops out of use.

5 The harpsichord is replaced by the piano – capable of considerable powers of expression, including gradual *crescendo* or *diminuendo*, sudden contrasts between *forte* and *piano*, and between *staccato* (short, detached) and *legato* (smooth, flowing); early piano music often light and thinnish in texture (Haydn, Mozart), but later becoming richer, deeper-toned, more sonorous and powerful (Beethoven).

6 Instrumental music increases in importance; main types: the Classical sonata, symphony, concerto, trio and string quartet (chamber music), divertimento and serenade (often performed out of doors in the evening); main types of vocal music: the Mass, and opera.

7 Sonata form the most important musical form or structure – almost always used to build up the first movement of large-scale works; also sometimes used for other movements, and single pieces (e.g. overtures).

Making musical connections

🎧 60

Listen to part of the first movement of **Symphony No. 99 in E♭** by Haydn, composed in 1793 and first performed in London the following year. Haydn structures this movement in sonata form (see page 55), and you will hear the exposition section. Here is the first subject:

The bridge passage (which is rather lengthy) begins like this:

. . . and leads eventually to the second subject – played first by clarinet and violins, and then repeated (and decorated) by oboe and violins:

Now listen to the opening of Prokofiev's *Classical Symphony* (1916–17). The music is in **neoclassical style**: a 20th-century style in which the composer sets out to imitate aspects of the style and structures of the Classical period (or, sometimes, the Baroque period – e.g. the Stravinsky piece on page 47). Prokofiev commented that he composed his *Classical Symphony* 'as Haydn might have written it if he had lived in our day'.

🎧 61

The first movement is in sonata form, and you will hear the exposition section. Listen for the second subject – to be played 'with elegance':

Assignment 52

Listen again to the music by Haydn and Prokofiev. As you listen to each excerpt, note down which of the following items match the music you are hearing. (An item may match one extract only, or both – or neither.)

> (a) the first subject is played *piano*, then repeated *forte*
> (b) 2 beats to a bar
> (c) 4 beats to a bar
> (d) fairly lively tempo (speed)
> (e) lazy, moderate tempo
> (f) scored for standard 'Classical orchestra'
> (g) scored for large orchestra, with extra percussion
> (h) a 'tick-tocking' bassoon is featured in the accompaniment to the second subject
> (i) frequent sudden and surprising changes of key
> (j) harpsichord *continuo* used

Assignment 53

In the first movement of Beethoven's 'Eroica' Symphony, one of the most characteristic features which has great impact is the rhythmic effect called *syncopation*. Listen to how the 20th-century Hungarian composer, Bartók, uses syncopation with vigorous and exciting effect in the second movement of his ***Music for Strings, Percussion and Celesta***. The bowed string instruments are divided into two equal and opposing orchestras, separated to left and to right on the concert platform, with harp, percussion and celesta positioned in the middle:

double basses I				double basses II
cellos I	kettle drums	tam-tam	bass drum	cellos II
violas I	celesta	snare drums	cymbals	violas II
violins II			xylophone	violins IV
violins I	piano		harp	violins III
		conductor		

⏵⏵ 62 Here are a few of the many occasions during this excerpt when you will hear syncopation (see if you can spot other instances for yourself). The time signature is $\frac{2}{4}$ throughout, except for two single bars of $\frac{3}{4}$.

0'16"   piano enters – then, short quaver patterns (violins III and I alternately) arguing against the beat, followed by a syncopated pattern on kettle drums;

1'21"   rising patterns beginning with an accent on the last quaver of a bar ('off' the beat), and then with accents shifting – those of orchestra I arguing against those of orchestra II;

2'23"   strings and celesta play two-note patterns (accents not always coinciding with the beat) – leading to crashing chords, violently syncopated;

2'48"   against a web of quavers featuring the harp: dry, syncopated chords (quite unpredictable) played on piano, *pizzicato* strings and, later, xylophone and snare drum.

One of the most typical features of Beethoven's style is the use of strong musical contrasts. This is also an important feature of much Balinese gamelan music. A *gamelan* is an Indonesian orchestra or instrumental ensemble. The instruments most commonly used include:

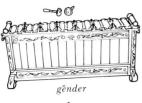

gĕnder

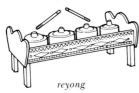

reyong

kĕndang

- metallophones, of two types: *saron*, and *gĕnder* (similar to a xylophone);
- suspended gongs, of different sizes and pitches;
- gong-chimes (sets of knobbed gong kettles) of two main kinds: *trompong*, and *reyong*;
- cymbals: *ceng-ceng*;
- drums: *kĕndang* (double-headed drums, played in pairs).

Also sometimes included are: *suling*, a bamboo flute; *rabāb*, a two-string spike-fiddle; and *guntang*, a one-string bamboo tube zither.

The drummers lead the ensemble, and give musical signals indicating changes in tempo (speed), and dynamic level (volume of sound).

The music of a Balinese composition is based upon a main melody, called the *pokok* (a 'fixed' melody, or 'nuclear' melody). This is played in long notes by the lower-sounding instruments, and punctuated by one or more gongs. Above and around the main melody, higher-sounding instruments play different variations on the same melody in various degrees of intricacy – so creating a *heterophonic* musical texture. Generally, the higher the pitch of the instrument, the more rapid and intricate are the note-patterns it plays.

Investigate an excerpt from a Balinese dance called ***Tamulilingan***, which means 'Bumblebees'. This music has been described as 'pure and mysterious like moonlight – always the same and yet always changing, like a running stream'. The music is structured from a pentatonic scale, called *sělisir* – shown on the left, with approximate pitches.

Assignment 54

63 First, listen to *Tamulilingan* simply to enjoy the varied and colourful sounds of the Balinese gamelan. Then listen again, noting down all the different kinds of musical *contrast* which you notice.

Assignment 55

The music below is also based on the Balinese *sělisir* scale – but here transposed to begin on E (as shown below, on the left). The music on the lower stave is the *pokok* (main, fixed melody). The music on the upper stave is a decorated variation of the main melody. Notice that each four-note pattern includes the main melody note at least once.

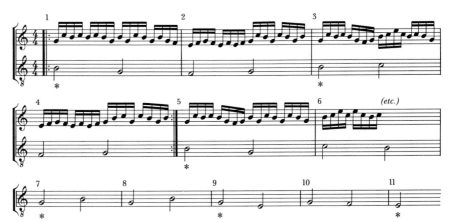

[* = a stroke on gong or cymbal, and/or the note sounded and sustained on a low-sounding instrument.]

1 Form a small group and, using any suitable instruments, play bars 1–4 two or three times. (If you are using xylophones or glockenspiels, first remove, if possible, all notes except those of the *sělisir* scale shown on the left.) Discuss and decide: tempo, and dynamic level.

2 Compose/improvise a continuation of the decorated variation of the main melody. You could end at bar 11 – or carry on further, choosing your own notes to continue the main melody.

3 Make a recording of the complete piece; then listen to it and discuss it. Afterwards, listen again to the extract from *Tamulilingan*.

Assignment 56

Listen again to the slow movement of Mozart's Clarinet Concerto (composed in 1791, the last year of his life). Then listen to the first movement of Stravinsky's ***Ebony Concerto*** for clarinet and jazz band, composed in 1945 for the jazz clarinettist, Woody Herman, and his band. (The title comes from 'ebony stick', the jazz term for clarinet.)

These two movements, from clarinet concertos composed more than a century and a half apart, are strongly contrasted in sound and musical style. Describe the differences you notice. For instance, consider: rhythm, timbres/instrumentation, harmony, melody, any special instrumental effects, treatment of the solo clarinet, texture.

Assignment 57

In most pieces or movements by Baroque composers, the same mood is kept throughout, and also the same rhythm. A composer of the Classical period structures a piece by using contrasting tunes and rhythms, with the mood constantly changing, emphasized by frequent changes of timbre.

Some pieces of rock music keep the same mood and style throughout. But listen to a piece in which rhythm, timbres, textures, mood and style are all frequently changing: '**Bohemian Rhapsody**' by the British rock group, **Queen**. Here is a skeleton plan of the piece:

Freddie Mercury of Queen

0'00"	(a)	Introduction (14 bars);
0'48"	(b)	Verse 1 – 'Mama, just killed a man . . .', with piano accompaniment, lowest notes reinforced by bass guitar;
1'46"	(c)	Verse 2 – 'Too late, my time has come . . .'
2'35"	(d)	Instrumental break (8 bars);
3'00"	(e)	Verse 3 – introduced by *staccato* chords;
4'04"	(f)	Verse 4 – 'So you think you can stone me . . .'
4'33"	(g)	Instrumental break – the music eventually slowing down;
5'08"	(h)	Coda – 'Nothing really matters . . .'

1 Listen to 'Bohemian Rhapsody', especially noticing changes in mood and style.
2 Then listen again, discovering answers to these questions, one on each section of the piece.
   (a) Are the first few bars performed by: solo voice with guitars; several voices unaccompanied; or two voices and synthesizer?
   (b) Which of these patterns matches the piano accompaniment in the first part of verse 1?

   (c) The melody of verse 2 is basically the same as that of verse 1 – but what differences are there in the accompaniment/backing?
   (d) Name the instrument featured mostly in the instrumental break.
   (e) Mention some of the ways in which excitement is built up during verse 3.
   (f) Which of these describes the style of verse 4?
        blues;   reggae;   heavy rock;   ragtime.
   (g) Which instrument is featured in the instrumental break?
   (h) How does the material of the coda give *balance* to the whole song?

Romantic Expansion 1810~1910

During the 19th century, described as the Romantic period, the range of musical materials used by composers expanded enormously. Romantic composers looked for a greater freedom in the design and structure of their music, and a more intense and personal expression of emotion. Melodies became more lyrical and song-like, with more adventurous modulations (changes of key). Harmonies became richer, with a more powerful use of discords, bringing in chromatic notes from outside the key (*chromatic* is from a Greek word which means 'coloured'). Musical textures became fuller and denser, often weighty. The piano was improved and developed, and there was an increase in the size of the orchestra, offering composers a far wider range in pitch, volume, and timbres.

The music of the Romantics offers a rich variety of types of composition, ranging from works for just one or a few performers, such as piano pieces, songs and chamber music, to huge musical canvases, structured on a large time-scale and requiring an enormous number of musicians, such as the operas (music dramas) of Wagner and the lengthy orchestral works of Berlioz, Mahler, and Richard Strauss.

Closer links between music and art and literature sparked off a keener interest in composing programme music (descriptive music) - especially symphonic poems. There were rapid advancements in performing technique, particularly among pianists and violinists, and audiences idolized virtuoso performers such as Liszt and Paganini.

Among the ideas which fascinated and inspired Romantic composers are:

- nature and the seasons; rivers, lakes and forests;
- night, moonlight, and dreams;
- myths, legends and fairy-tales;
- mystery, magic and the supernatural;
- far-off lands and the distant past;
- the joy and pain of love - especially young love.

Timechart: 19th-century Romantic composers

| | 1810 | 1820 | 1830 | 1840 | **1850** | 1860 | 1870 | 1880 | 1890 | **1900** | 1910 |

Beethoven Germany 1770–1827

Weber Germany 1786–1826

Rossini Italy 1792–1868

Schubert Austria 1797–1828

Berlioz France 1803–1869

Mendelssohn Germany 1809–1847

Chopin Poland 1810–1849

Schumann Germany 1810–1856

Liszt Hungary 1811–1886

Wagner Germany 1813–1883

Verdi Italy 1813–1901

Smetana Bohemia 1824–1884

Bruckner Austria 1824–1896

J. Strauss II Austria 1825–1899

Brahms Germany 1833–1897

Saint-Saëns France 1835–1921

Bizet France 1838–1875

Russia 1839–1881 **Musorgsky**

Tchaikovsky Russia 1840–1893

Dvořák Bohemia 1841–1904

Grieg Norway 1843–1907

Rimsky-Korsakov Russia 1844–1908

Elgar England 1857–1934

Puccini Italy 1858–1924

Albéniz Spain 1860–1909

Mahler Austria 1860–1911

Delius England 1862–1934

R. Strauss Germany 1864–1949

| | 1810 | 1820 | 1830 | 1840 | **1850** | 1860 | 1870 | 1880 | 1890 | **1900** | 1910 |

(page 63) The legend of the minotaur (part man, part bull); romantic conductor; a Greek folly; symbol of Freedom; Arabian camels; (this page) air balloon flight; an early automobile, manufactured by Benz; building the first railways.

The German *Lied*

Lied is the German word for 'song'. Musicians use this word to refer, in particular, to the 19th-century German **Lied** for solo voice and piano (the plural is **Lieder**). In most Lieder, the piano part is much more than just a 'prop' for the voice. Instead, voice and piano are treated as equal partners – the piano often setting the mood, and perhaps adding dramatic or pictorial detail. Sometimes a composer writes a **song-cycle** - setting a whole group of poems linked to the same idea, perhaps even outlining a story. The first great Romantic composer of Lieder was Schubert, who wrote more than 600.

Listen to a Lied by Schubert called '**Der stürmische Morgen**' (The Stormy Morning). It is one of the 24 songs, setting poems by Wilhelm Müller, which make up his song-cycle entitled *Winterreise* (Winter Journey) composed in 1827. This song-cycle sketches the story of a young man who, disappointed in love and troubled in mind, decides to journey through the bleak winter countryside. The recording of 'Der stürmische Morgen' on the cassette is by Peter Pears (tenor) and Benjamin Britten (piano).

⊙⊙ 65 **Assignment 58** First, read through the words. Then listen to the recording. Notice how Schubert varies the style of the piano part in this short song. (Schubert marks the music to be performed 'rather swift, yet vigorously'.)

Assignment 59

(a) In which key does this song begin and end?

(b) What musical differences are there between the beginning of verse 1 and the beginning of verse 2?

(c) At which words in the poem/translation does the climax occur? How is this emphasized in the piano part?

(d) How does Schubert create a wild and stormy mood in this song?

Music for piano

The **piano** was the most popular instrument of the Romantic period. During the first half of the 19th century, several improvements were made and the number of notes was increased – giving the piano a richer, fuller sound and a wider range in pitch, tone and volume.

Among the types of composition by Romantic composers, involving piano, were: sonatas – for solo piano, or piano with one other instrument; chamber works; songs; concertos – the piano in opposition to the full orchestra; and a great variety of individual pieces for solo piano. These included:

- dances, such as the waltz, mazurka, polonaise;
- 'mood' or 'character' pieces, such as the ballade, rhapsody, romance, impromptu (meaning 'on the spur of the moment', 'as if improvised'), prelude, nocturne ('night-piece'), and étude ('study').

The Romantic composer who showed the deepest understanding of the piano's character and capabilities was Fryderyk Chopin. Typical of his style is an expressive melody, played *cantabile* ('in a singing style'), above a flowing accompaniment. Listen to Chopin's **Étude in E major**, Opus 10 No. 3. An étude is intended to improve a performer's ability in some way – and so presents the player with a technical challenge. Chopin's 27 études certainly do that, but they also rely on musical, expressive qualities. 'Every one a poem!' wrote the German composer, Schumann, when he first heard them. Chopin structures this particular Étude in ternary form (A^1 B A^2), with a short link joining B and A^2, and a coda to round off. Section B brings in many *chromatic* notes (notes from outside the key).

Assignment 60

Follow the score as the recording is played, listening on when the printed music ends. Notice where A^1 ends and section B begins. And listen for when the opening music returns later as A^2.

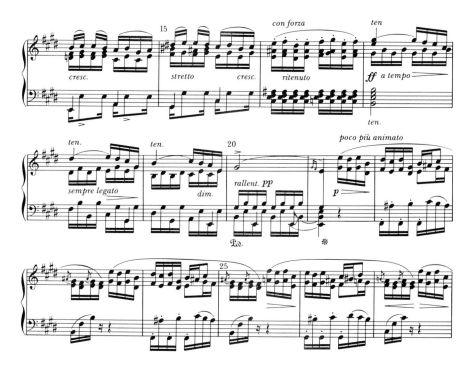

Assignment 61

1 (a) In which bar of the opening section (A^1) does the climax occur?

(b) In which bar does the middle section (B) begin?

(c) Mention three ways in which music B presents contrast to music A.

(d) When music A returns after music B, Chopin omits 8 of the original bars. Which bars are they?

(e) Does the coda use a new musical idea – or an idea heard previously?

2 (a) Which music – A, or B – do you think presents most challenge to the performer?

(b) In which section – A^1, B, or A^2 – does the main climax occur?

(c) In this Étude, which of the following are most important?

melody; rhythm; harmony; counterpoint.

The expansion of the orchestra

During the Romantic period there was an expansion in the range and size of the **orchestra** – sometimes to huge proportions.

- the brass section, soon completed by the addition of the tuba, becomes much more important, more weighty and sonorous – its range and flexibility greatly increased by the invention of the valve system; typically, the section now includes: 4 horns, 3 trumpets, 3 trombones and tuba;

- composers sometimes write for woodwind instruments in threes or even fours, adding the four 'extra' woodwinds: piccolo, cor anglais, bass clarinet, and double bassoon – so extending the section's range in pitch, volume, and timbre;

- the choice of percussion instruments becomes more varied and colourful;

- the number of string players has to be increased to maintain a balance of sound between the four orchestral sections;

- sometimes one (or more than one) harp is also included.

Listen to 'Siegfried's Funeral March' from Wagner's opera *Götterdämmerung* – the fourth and final opera in his cycle called *The Ring of the Nibelung* which he intended to be performed on four successive evenings. The large orchestra needed to perform this funeral march is shown at the top of the opposite page.

Wagner's operas are lengthy works, with the music spun continuously from beginning to end of each act. Woven into the texture are many, usually short, themes known as **leading-motives**. Each one represents a character, or an object (e.g. the Sword, the Ring), an idea or an emotion, or a place. During an opera, Wagner continually develops these symbolic musical ideas, changing and transforming them according to the situation at the time. The leading-motive shown as A, below, is Siegfried's horn-call. B shows it transformed to become Siegfried, the Hero. C is a further transformation, heard during *Siegfried's Funeral March*. (You will hear yet another transformation at the close of the march.)

A  B  C

Assignment 62

The main leading-motives heard during *Siegfried's Funeral March* are printed opposite – in the form in which they are originally heard during *The Ring* cycle. Some will be transformed (altered) as they appear during the march.

The Volsungs are the offspring of Wotan, ruler of the gods. They include Siegmund and Sieglinde – Siegfried's father and mother. Brünnhilde is a Valkyrie (warrior daughter of Wotan) and has fallen in love with Siegfried.

〇〇 67   As you listen to *Siegfried's Funeral March*, match the eleven motives against the plan of the piece, printed beneath them. Also notice:
- the powerful climaxes;
- the wide range in pitch, volume, and timbres;
- varied textures;
- rich harmonies (often chromatic).

Assignment 63

Listen to the music again, discovering answers to these questions:
(a) Describe the two musical ideas which make up motive 1 (Death).
(b) The short motive 4 (Sieglinde) is played three times by different instruments. Arrange them in the order you hear them:
  clarinet;   oboe and horn;   cor anglais.
(c) The music builds to its first climax, at which motive 6 (The Sword) is heard. Which instrument plays it?
(d) A transformation of motive 1 (Death) immediately follows. What main change does Wagner make to it?
(e) The music builds to its second climax. Which motive is heard as this climax is reached?
(f) Which of these combinations of timbres plays motive 9 (Brünnhilde)?

| clarinet + cor anglais | tenor tuba + piccolo | oboe + trombone |

(g) How does Wagner make motive 10 (the Power of the Ring) sound sinister and menacing?
(h) Describe how Wagner transforms motive 8 (Siegfried, the Hero) when it is heard at the close of the funeral march.

Wagner's orchestra for *Siegfried's Funeral March*:

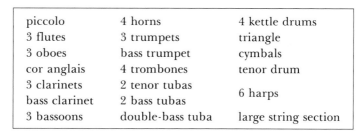

piccolo	4 horns	4 kettle drums
3 flutes	3 trumpets	triangle
3 oboes	bass trumpet	cymbals
cor anglais	4 trombones	tenor drum
3 clarinets	2 tenor tubas	6 harps
bass clarinet	2 bass tubas	
3 bassoons	double-bass tuba	large string section

These eleven leading-motives are heard during the March:

During *Siegfried's Funeral March*, the eleven leading-motives are heard in this order:

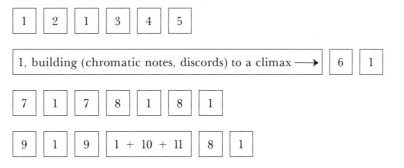

| 1 | 2 | 1 | 3 | 4 | 5 |

| 1, building (chromatic notes, discords) to a climax ⟶ | 6 | 1 |

| 7 | 1 | 7 | 8 | 1 | 8 | 1 |

| 9 | 1 | 9 | 1 + 10 + 11 | 8 | 1 |

A nationalist symphonic poem

During the Romantic period, closer links between music and art and literature caused a keener interest in the composing of **programme music** – music which attempts to 'tell a story', or is in some way descriptive, so that it conjures up images in the mind of the listener. Three main types of programme music for orchestra are:

- the programme symphony – e.g. Berlioz's *Symphonie Fantastique*;
- the concert overture – e.g. Mendelssohn's *The Hebrides (Fingal's Cave)*;
- the symphonic poem (also called tone poem).

Investigate excerpts from Musorgsky's symphonic poem, **Night on the Bare Mountain**. Musorgsky was one of a group of Russian composers who became known as 'The Russian Five' (the other four were Rimsky-Korsakov, Borodin, Balakirev, and Cui). Their aim was to break free from the powerful musical influences of German composers, and to discover a distinctive musical style which would be expressive and characteristic of their own nationality. Composers of other countries were also fired by the same spirit – for example, Smetana in Bohemia, Grieg in Norway. This led to a brand of Romanticism which is called **nationalism**. The chief ways in which composers may give their works a nationalist flavour are:

- by using melodic and rhythmic features of their country's folk-music;
- by using scenes from their country's life, history, folk-tales and legends as a basis for operas, songs, and symphonic poems.

Musorgsky's symphonic poem, *Night on the Bare Mountain*, paints a vivid orchestral picture of a witches' sabbath which, in Russian folk-lore, takes place on Bare Mountain, near Kiev, on St John's Eve (Midsummer's Eve). Four excerpts from the symphonic poem are recorded on the cassette (you will hear the music in Rimsky-Korsakov's brilliant arrangement). Brief descriptions of the excerpts, together with the main themes, are printed opposite.

The witches' sabbath

◯◯ 68   **1** Mysterious and ominous sounds from the strings, then shrill woodwinds, set the mood.

A 

Brass instruments announce the appearance of spirits and demons.

B 

A rumble of thunder, and flashes of lightning . . .

◯◯ 69   **2** The demons begin a dance, which eventually becomes wilder.

C 

A sudden pause – then witches arrive, to prepare a Black Mass in hommage to the Devil.

D 

◯◯ 70   **3** The Black Mass is celebrated – the music building to a climax marked by a dramatic crash on a tam-tam. A swift *diminuendo*, and a distant church clock strikes six . . .

◯◯ 71   **4** In the coda which ends the piece, a calm melody suggests a shepherd playing his pipe as dawn breaks on Bare Mountain.

E 

Assignment 64   Listen to the four excerpts again, answering these questions:

1 (a) Which brass instruments play theme B?
  (b) How are the effects of thunder and lightning portrayed in the music?

2 (a) How is theme C often given the effect of syncopation?
  (b) Which section of the orchestra plays theme D?
  (c) Do tempo and dynamics remain the same throughout this second excerpt, or do they change?

3 (a) With which of the themes does this third excerpt begin?
  (b) How is excitement built up during the music of this excerpt?

4 (a) Which two instruments, in turn, play theme E?
  (b) How are the first two bars of the melody different when the second instrument plays them?
  (c) Describe the mood of the music in this fourth excerpt.

Assignment 65   1 Listen to a complete recording of Musorgsky's *Night on the Bare Mountain* in Rimsky-Korsakov's arrangement.

2 Then (if possible) compare it with a recording of Musorgsky's own, original version – which is, in fact, very different indeed.

Fingerprints of musical style

The main characteristics of Romantic music (1810–1910)

1 A more intense and personal expression of feelings and emotions, with fantasy and imagination playing an important part; a greater freedom in musical form and design; works structured on a larger time-scale.

2 Melodies, whether tender or passionate, become more lyrical and song-like; harmonies become richer, often chromatic, with striking use of discords, and swift and adventurous modulations.

3 Musical textures become denser and weightier, exploring a wider range of pitch, dynamics, and timbres, often with bold dramatic contrasts.

4 An expansion in the range and size of the orchestra – sometimes to huge proportions; the brass section, its range and flexibility now increased by the invention of the valve system, gains in importance and often dominates the texture.

5 A rich and wide variety of types of composition – ranging from works for just one or a few performers (piano pieces, songs, chamber music) to works demanding an enormous number of musicians, and structured with spectacular dramatic and dynamic climaxes.

6 Closer links with art and literature lead to a keen interest in composing programme music (symphonic poem, concert overture, programme symphony).

7 Composers sometimes bring shape and unity to lengthy works by the use of recurring themes and motives, often transformed in mood and character as they reappear – e.g. thematic transformation (Liszt), leading-motive (Wagner).

8 Greater technical virtuosity – especially from pianists and violinists, and exploited particularly in concertos.

9 Nationalism – a reaction against the dominating influences of German music by composers of other nationalities (especially Russian and Czech).

| **Making musical connections** | Musorgsky's symphonic poem *Night on the Bare Mountain* is vividly programmatic (descriptive). Here is another piece of *programme music* - very different in style and timbre. Many instrumental pieces by Japanese composers are programmatic - often with evocative titles, such as *Plum Blossoms, Waves on the Shore, Windsong, Moon and Cloud, Winter Morning*. |

🔊 72　　Listen to **Ballad of the Snowstorm** by Katsutoshi Nagasawa. The piece is played by an ensemble of Japanese instruments, including:

- *shakuhachi* - an end-blown flute with only four finger-holes and one thumb-hole but, by means of special fingering and blowing techniques, capable of a range of three octaves;
- *biwa* - a pear-shaped plucked lute, with four or five strings;
- *shamisen* - a long-necked plucked lute, with three strings;
- *koto* - a long zither with 13 strings, equal in length, thickness and tension, and 13 movable bridges;
- *taiko* - a shallow barrel drum played with two wooden sticks.

shamisen

taiko

koto

shakuhachi

biwa

Assignment 66　During *Ballad of the Snowstorm* there are several changes of mood and tempo. Listen to the piece again. Describe the opening music (25 seconds or so). Then describe the changes which take place.

Assignment 67　Form a group of musicians, and compose/improvise a short programmatic piece. Choose one of the titles mentioned above - or think up an idea/title of your own. Then decide:

which instruments to select which will offer suitable timbres to match your 'programme';

whether, in structuring your piece, it would be best to keep the same mood throughout, or to have some (perhaps dramatic) changes of mood, tempo, dynamics, and so on.

Record your piece. Then listen to it and discuss it.

Assignment 68　The music of Japan has been greatly influenced by that of other cultures, including China, Korea, and - more recently - the West. If possible, listen to some of these compositions by 20th-century Japanese composers:

Toru Takemitsu: *Green (November Steps II)* for orchestra; *Cassiopeia* for solo percussionist and orchestra (the soloist plays from a graphic score which calls for much improvisation); *Water Music*, a 'musique concrète' piece consisting entirely of manipulated sounds of water-drops.

Maki Ishii: *Sō-Gū II* - consisting of simultaneous performances of 'Music for Gagaku' (for Japanese instrumental ensemble) and 'Sō' for orchestra.

One of the greatest virtuoso pianists of the Romantic period was the Hungarian composer, Franz Liszt. A *virtuoso* is a musician of extraordinary technical skill. And so dazzlingly brilliant were Liszt's skills at the piano that many people thought that he (and also the violinist, Paganini) had made a pact with the Devil!

Investigate four excerpts from Liszt's **Piano Concerto No. 1 in E♭ major**. The work is structured in a single movement in four linked sections, and Liszt uses the device which he called *thematic transformation*. Throughout the Concerto, themes reappear – but are often transformed in mood and character. The transformations may include changes of: melodic shape, rhythm, speed, dynamics, timbre, and style of accompaniment.

In excerpts 1–3 on the cassette, you will hear the opening theme of each of the first three sections of the Concerto. Excerpt 1 also includes the pianist's first *cadenza* – an unaccompanied, showy passage displaying the player's technique.

Listen to excerpts 1–3, two or three times, to fix these important themes in your mind.

Assignment 69 (a) In the first excerpt: what is the melodic range, in semitones, of the theme?
(b) Which of the following matches the style and mood of excerpt 2?

| march | nocturne | waltz | polonaise |

(c) In excerpt 3 another instrument is featured besides the piano. Which one? (Liszt was strongly criticized for including this instrument at all in a concerto.)

76 Now listen to excerpt 4, from the final section of the Concerto. You will hear, at various times, themes 1–3 (above), and also this new theme – though the opening notes outline the pitches of theme 1.

Assignment 70   Listen to the fourth excerpt two or three times more.

1 Notice the virtuoso style of piano writing and piano playing. For example:
- passages in swift notes – often based on scales, arpeggios, and broken chords;
- swiftly repeated notes;
- chromatic passages – including all twelve notes of the chromatic scale;
- trills, and tremolos;
- splashing chords, played *sforzando*;
- *bravura* octaves and double octaves – octaves in each hand (*bravura* is an Italian word meaning 'skill', and also 'bravery'!)

Notice also the wide range used of the piano – low to high; and the solo piano, when required, holding its own against the full orchestra.

2 (a) Which of the four themes printed opposite do you hear first in this excerpt? In what ways is it transformed (changed) from its original appearance?

(b) Which instruments first play theme 4? And which instruments play it when it is immediately repeated?

3 Make a list of all the appearances in this excerpt of the four themes, in the order in which you hear them.

Assignment 71   If possible, listen to a recording of the complete Concerto. And then, perhaps, compare it with a piano concerto by a Classical composer such as Mozart or Haydn, and a 20th-century piano concerto such as Bartók's Piano Concerto No. 3, Prokofiev's Piano Concerto No. 3, Stravinsky's Concerto for piano and wind instruments, or the imaginative and exciting Piano Concerto No. 1 by the Argentine composer, Alberto Ginastera (try, for example, the fourth movement which is a very rhythmic and exhilarating *Toccata concertata*).

'Liszt at the piano': a painting by Joseph Dannhauser, showing (from left to right) Alexandre Dumas, Victor Hugo, George Sand, Paganini with Rossini, Liszt, and the Countess Marie d'Agoult (the bust is of Beethoven).

Assignment 72   Listen again to Chopin's Étude in E major. Then compare it with two rather different keyboard pieces – one by a Baroque composer, the other by a 20th-century composer.

1   First listen to **Sonata in A major** (Kk24; L495) by Domenico Scarlatti. He composed around 550 single-movement sonatas for harpsichord, all of them in binary form (in two sections of music: A, and B). Scarlatti was a virtuoso harpsichordist. And this Sonata includes several features of his brilliant keyboard style: swiftly-repeated notes, often shared between the two hands; flashing scale passages; spicy discords; and very effective passages for crossing hands (Scarlatti became annoyed as he grew older – and fatter – to find that he could no longer manage to play these).

Here are six main musical ideas on which this Sonata is based. (L = left hand; R = right hand.)

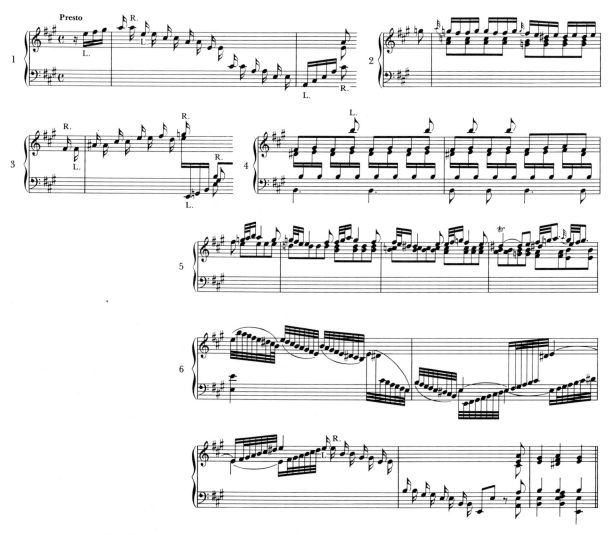

77   As you listen to the Sonata, spot these six main ideas during section A. Then note down the order in which they reappear during section B. (The recording on the cassette is without repeats.)

2 Now investigate an excerpt from a piece very different in sound and style: **Interlude 1** from *Sonatas and Interludes for prepared piano* by the American composer, John Cage. The whole work includes 16 Sonatas (each in binary form like those of Scarlatti) and 4 Interludes. Before a performance of this music, the piano must be 'prepared' – nuts, bolts and screws, pieces of rubber and plastic, must be fixed between, and under and over, certain strings in the piano. This affects the pitches, and also considerably alters the timbres, according to the materials used.

⏹ 78   Listen for: richly varied sonorities, sometimes resembling Eastern bells, gongs, and drums; musical ideas, motives and patterns often repeated; intriguing rhythmic effects.

Assignment 73   Listen to the Balinese gamelan piece, *Tamulilingan* (page 61). Then listen again to Cage's *Interlude 1*. Mention any similarities that you notice.

Assignment 74   Compose an experimental piece for piano, for two or more performers.

1 Your piece could be for 'prepared' piano, using some of Cage's ideas. First decide which notes to prepare.
Discuss, and then try out, various ways of preparing them. For example, experiment with: erasers (rubbers); strips of rubber threaded through certain strings; nuts and bolts; screws or nails hanging loosely between strings; paper clips hanging from strings.
  Also, try moving materials to different positions along the strings, judging the effect. But, *at all times*, take great care not to damage the piano in any way.

2 Instead (or perhaps as well) you could include some playing techniques used by another American composer, Henry Cowell, in his piano pieces. Here is a selection:

- On the keyboard (varying the dynamics) press down notes with:
  (a) the flat of the hand;
  (b) a lightly-clenched fist;
  (c) the entire forearm.

- *Inside* the piano (sustaining pedal down always):
  (a) pluck certain strings with the fingertip, fingernail, or some kind of plectrum (try different registers – and different positions along the strings);
  (b) sweep across the strings of several neighbouring notes, with the flesh of the finger, or the back of the fingernail;
  (c) sweep along the length of the string(s) of one or more notes.

Experiment, and discover other sounds, timbres and effects for yourself. Organize and structure your chosen sounds into a composition. Perform it, and record it. Then discuss it.

Assignment 75   If possible, listen to the following pieces:
Cowell: *Tiger*, and *The Banshee* (played entirely *inside* the piano);
Cage: *Amores* – two prepared piano solos framing two percussion trios.

Assignment 76   1 Listen to another Lied (song) by Schubert, called ***Am Meer*** (By the Sea), setting words by the German poet, Heine. Here is a translation:

 79

> 1 Far out upon the spacious sea
>   the sunset's rays were shining;
>   we sat by the fisherman's lonely hut,
>   we sat alone and were silent.
>
> 2 The mist arose, the waters swelled,
>   the seagull skimmed high above us;
>   and from your eyes so full of love,
>   tear-drops were gently falling.
>
> 3 I saw them falling upon your hand,
>   and then I knelt before you;
>   and from your white and trembling hand
>   I drank those falling tear-drops.
>
> 4 And since that moment my body's consumed,
>   my soul dies of desiring.
>   That woman, weeping and forlorn,
>   has poisoned me with her sad tears.

2 Listen to *Am Meer* again, answering these questions:
  (a) Is the first chord you hear a concord, or a discord?
  (b) Is verse 1 in a major key, or in a minor key?
  (c) How does the piano part set the mood and atmosphere for the opening words of verse 2?
  (d) Does verse 2 end with a perfect cadence, or with an imperfect cadence?
  (e) Is the music of verse 3 exactly the same as verse 1 – or is it very different from verse 1?
  (f) The climax of the whole song occurs in verse 4. At which words?
  (g) Comment on the ending of the song, played by the piano alone.

Assignment 77   Listen to songs – 20th-century word-settings – by two heavy rock groups:

'**The Rain Song**' (Jimmy Page/Robert Plant) performed by **Led Zeppelin**, on the album *Houses of the Holy*; also on *The Song Remains the Same*

80 '**Paranoid**' (Iommi/Osbourne/Butler/Ward) performed by **Black Sabbath**

These two songs achieve impact in different ways, and by different musical means. For example, one of them makes its effect within a narrow range of harmonies; the other uses a wide range of harmonies (sometimes chromatic).

1 Listen to these two songs (two or three times, in alternation), and compare them. Comment on the differences between them with regard to:

| melody (and melodic range) | harmonies | rhythm | tempo |

| use of timbres (instrumental, and vocal) |

2 For each song:
  (a) describe what you think the mood is;
  (b) mention the musical ingredient(s) used *mostly* to achieve the mood and the overall effect.

20th-century Exploration

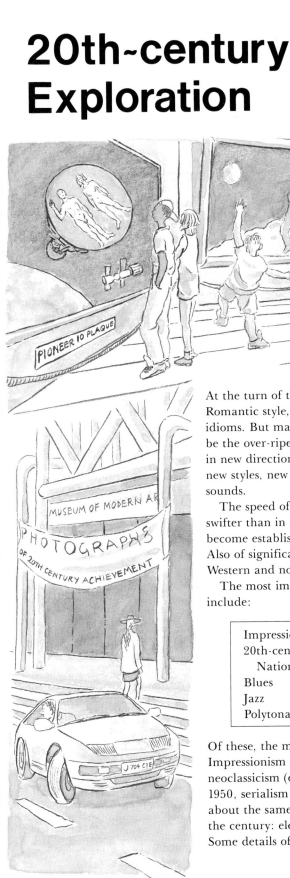

At the turn of the century, some composers continued to write in a warm Romantic style, mainly using traditional techniques, and perhaps national idioms. But many others, now strongly reacting to what they considered to be the over-ripe and excessive style of late Romanticism, chose to strike out in new directions. Exploration and experiment led to a fascinating variety of new styles, new trends, new techniques and, in some cases, entirely new sounds.

The speed of change in Western music during the 20th century has been swifter than in any previous period – at times, a new trend has hardly become established before another has appeared and claimed attention. Also of significance has been the two-way musical influence between Western and non-Western cultures.

The most important styles, trends, and techniques in 20th-century music include:

Impressionism	Expressionism	Musique concrète
20th-century	Atonality	Electronic music
Nationalism	Pointillism	Total serialism
Blues	Neoclassicism	Rock and Pop
Jazz	Serialism	Aleatory music
Polytonality	Microtonality	

Of these, the most significant during the first half of the century were Impressionism (see page 82), Expressionism and atonality (page 85), neoclassicism (example on page 59, also page 47), and serialism. Around 1950, serialism again came to the fore. And two other trends, originating at about the same time, have remained important during the second half of the century: electronic music (example on pages 87–89), and aleatory music. Some details of serialism and aleatory music are given on the next page.

Serialism, or 'Twelve-note' music

A procedure or technique of composing devised by Schoenberg, around 1920.

- first, the composer arranges all twelve notes of the chromatic scale in any chosen order; this becomes the basic *series* (note-row, basic set) on which the entire composition will be based;
- as well as using the series in this *original* form, the composer may use it in *retrograde* (the notes in reverse order), or *inversion* (the series turned upside down), or *retrograde inversion* (backwards and upside down at the same time);
- any of these forms of the series may be transposed – to begin on any note of the chromatic scale;
- forms of the series may be used horizontally as melodic lines (which may be woven together in counterpoint), or notes may be stacked vertically to structure chords/harmonies;
- all twelve notes are equally important; none should appear 'out of turn' (though a note may be immediately repeated); but any note may appear at any octave;
- the composer must use skill, imagination and musicianship in shaping melodic lines from the various forms of the series, in constructing chords, applying rhythm, selecting timbres, deciding upon dynamics and expression, and creating textures.

In the early 1950s, some composers (e.g. Boulez, Stockhausen) experimented in **total serialism**, in which twelve-element series of pitches, and also of durations (note-values), dynamics, attack (touch, articulation), tempos, and timbres, may be totally controlled by Schoenberg's principle of serialism. An example of total serialism is Stockhausen's *Gruppen* (page 32). On the left, you can see Stockhausen's basic series for the piece.

Aleatory music (depending upon chance or choice)

While total serialism offers the composer tighter control, **aleatory music** (from Latin, *alea*: 'a dice') makes for greater freedom by involving a degree of chance, choice, indeterminacy or unpredictability – either in the composing process, in performance, or in both. Some possibilities are:

- the composer may take decisions about which notes to use and how to use them by throwing a dice (or by some other chance operation);
- a performer may be asked to make a choice between several alternatives (e.g. which notes or which sections of the music to perform, and in which order);
- the pitch of notes may be precisely indicated (or merely suggested) but not their duration – or vice versa; decisions or choices may have to be taken about tempo (speed), dynamics, expression;
- the performer may be asked to improvise upon a given group of notes – or to improvise absolutely freely;
- for some aleatory pieces no musical notation may be provided at all – instead, a collection of symbols, a diagram, a drawing, perhaps a poem, or just a basic idea, to be freely and imaginatively interpreted.

Cage and Stockhausen have made much use of aleatory procedures in their music. The excerpts from the compositions by Tim Souster (page 87) and by Henze (page 94) include certain aleatory aspects.

Timechart: 20th-century composers

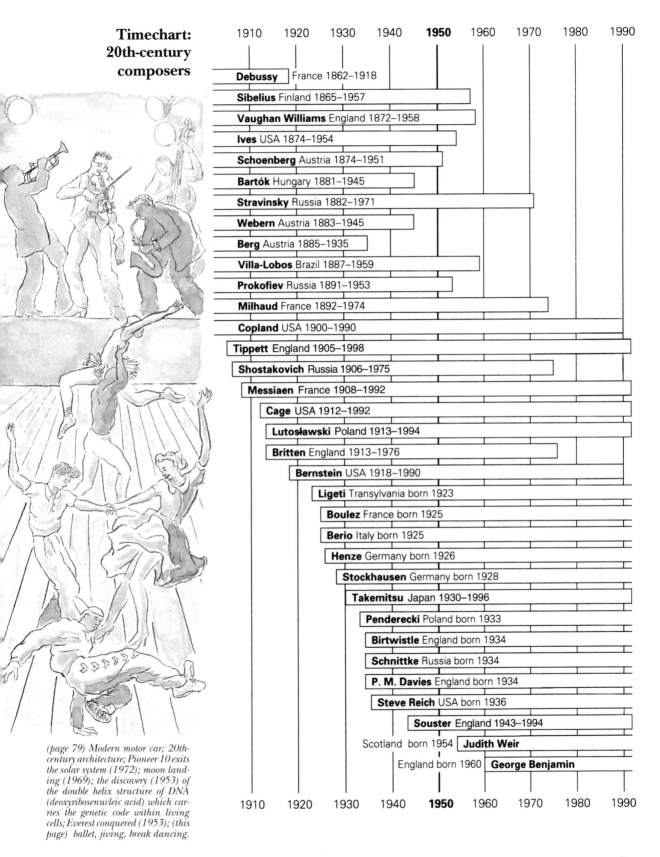

	1910	1920	1930	1940	**1950**	1960	1970	1980	1990

Debussy France 1862–1918

Sibelius Finland 1865–1957

Vaughan Williams England 1872–1958

Ives USA 1874–1954

Schoenberg Austria 1874–1951

Bartók Hungary 1881–1945

Stravinsky Russia 1882–1971

Webern Austria 1883–1945

Berg Austria 1885–1935

Villa-Lobos Brazil 1887–1959

Prokofiev Russia 1891–1953

Milhaud France 1892–1974

Copland USA 1900–1990

Tippett England 1905–1998

Shostakovich Russia 1906–1975

Messiaen France 1908–1992

Cage USA 1912–1992

Lutosławski Poland 1913–1994

Britten England 1913–1976

Bernstein USA 1918–1990

Ligeti Transylvania born 1923

Boulez France born 1925

Berio Italy born 1925

Henze Germany born 1926

Stockhausen Germany born 1928

Takemitsu Japan 1930–1996

Penderecki Poland born 1933

Birtwistle England born 1934

Schnittke Russia born 1934

P. M. Davies England born 1934

Steve Reich USA born 1936

Souster England 1943–1994

Scotland born 1954 **Judith Weir**

England born 1960 **George Benjamin**

	1910	1920	1930	1940	**1950**	1960	1970	1980	1990

(page 79) Modern motor car; 20th-century architecture; Pioneer 10 exits the solar system (1972); moon landing (1969); the discovery (1953) of the double helix structure of DNA (deoxyribosenucleic acid) which carries the genetic code within living cells; Everest conquered (1953); (this page) ballet, jiving, break dancing.

Impressionism This is a term borrowed from a style of painting used by a group of artists – mostly French – known as the Impressionists. They aimed for a greater naturalism in painting, and were particularly interested in depicting the effects of light and atmosphere. To achieve this, they used dabs of bright colour (shadows, too, taking on colour) and rather than producing a 'real', hard-edged effect, as in a photograph, they aimed to give an impression, such as the eye might take in at a single glance: an impression of hazy outlines, colour, atmosphere, and the play of shimmering light and movement.

In 20th-century music, the term **Impressionism** has been used to describe the style of certain composers – Debussy especially. As the Impressionist painters treated light and colour, so Debussy treated harmonies and timbres. Here are some characteristics of his 'Impressionist' style:

- the music is often programmatic (descriptive);
- chords (especially chromatic chords) are often used for their expressive 'colour' effects – rather than as part of a harmonic progression;
- discords may merge into further discords, similar chords (often 9ths, or 13ths) may flow in 'chord streams' in parallel motion – often giving a 'blurred' effect to the harmony;
- the use of unusual scales: modal scales, the five-note pentatonic scale, or the whole-tone scale (see page 8);
- often a vague, fluid, shifting quality in the music;
- exploration of unusual combinations of timbres, fluid rhythms, shimmering textures, subtle effects of light and shade;
- the music, though carefully structured, avoids hard clear-cut outlines – *suggesting* rather than stating.

'Waterlilies' by the Impressionist painter Claude Monet

Assignment 78   Listen to three excerpts from Debussy's piece called '**Nuages**' (Clouds), the first of his three orchestral *Nocturnes*, first performed in 1990.

 **81**   1 These four musical ideas are included in the first excerpt:

(a) Which sonorities (which instruments/timbres) does Debussy select for these ideas when each is first heard?

(b) During this music, are the strings muted, or unmuted?

 **82**   2 In the second excerpt listen for this melody, played by flute and harp:

(a) On which scale is this melody based – modal, pentatonic, or whole-tone?

(b) The melody is taken up by three other solo instruments. Are they:

> | violin, viola and cello |
>
> | clarinet, cor anglais and cello |
>
> | violin, oboe and saxophone |

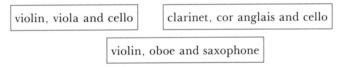 **83**   3 The third excerpt is the *coda*, which rounds off the piece. Which of the above musical ideas (A–E) reappear during the coda?

Assignment 79   Listen again to these three extracts from *Nuages*.

1   **melody** • **harmony** • **rhythm** • **timbre**

Do you think all the above ingredients are equally important in this music – or do some come over more noticeably than others?

2 Describe the mood or atmosphere conjured up by this music. What qualities or features in the music suggest this to you?

 **84   Assignment 80**   Now listen to part of a piano piece by Debussy called '**Reflets dans l'eau**' (Reflections in the water) from his first set of *Images* (1905). Listen especially for these three ideas:

What features and qualities of sound do you hear which identify this music as being in Debussy's 'Impressionist' style?

Stravinsky

One of the key figures in 20th-century music has been Igor Stravinsky. In his many compositions, he experimented with a wide range of modern styles and techniques, and his music has inspired and influenced countless other composers. One of his earlier works which had immense impact (it caused a riot in the audience when first performed!) was his 'pagan ballet' *The Rite of Spring* (1911–13). The music, which was described as 'savage primitivism', is written for a huge orchestra.

Listen to '**Dance of the Youths and Maidens**' from *The Rite of Spring*, following the music below. After bar 35, listen on – spotting appearances of the three tunes, A, B and C. Sometimes Stravinsky uses the technique of **polytonality** – the use of two (or more) keys at the same time. For instance, the opening harmony is constructed from a chord of Eb^7 sounding above a chord of Fb major (= E major).

Assignment 81

1 Name the instruments which first play each of the tunes, A, B and C.

2 The structure, and propulsion, of the music rely a great deal on the use of *ostinato* – a fairly short pattern of notes, persistently repeated. Write down the main ostinato pattern that you hear.

3 Which tune – A, B or C – is used to build the climax towards the end?

Assignment 82

Listen again to *Dance of the Youths and Maidens* – and for each of these categories, choose the description which best matches the music:

Melodic line:	long, flowing, unfolding	mainly made up of short fragments
Rhythm:	steady, smooth-flowing	often syncopated, with strong accents
Harmonies:	mainly discords	mainly concords
Dynamics:	mainly on one level, throughout	fairly wide range of dynamics
Mood:	excited, vigorous, exuberant	calm, relaxed, thoughtful
Timbres:	sharply contrasted, often vivid, clashing	mainly a blending of similar timbres
Texture:	dense, heavy throughout	many changes of texture

Expressionism

'Vision', painted by Arnold Schoenberg

Another term borrowed from painting – describing, in particular, the style of certain artists living in Vienna in the early 20th century. In their imaginative pictures they used distorted lines and vivid colours, often expressing their innermost experiences and exploring the darkest corners of the mind: secret terrors, and fantastic visions of the subconscious – sometimes suggesting mental breakdown. In music, **Expressionism** came to describe a style in which composers poured the most intense emotional expressiveness into their music. The most important composers who made use of Expressionist style were Schoenberg (who was also a painter) and his two pupils, Berg and Webern. At first, Expressionist music relied on harmonies which became more and more chromatic, eventually making free use of all twelve notes of the chromatic scale. This resulted in **atonality** – total absence of tonality, or key. Expressionist music in atonal style often features:

- extremely dissonant harmonies;
- frenzied, disjointed melodic lines, including wide leaps;
- violent, explosive contrasts;
- instruments often played forcefully at the extremes of their ranges;
- a high degree of tension – either vividly and dramatically portrayed, or 'lurking below the surface'.

A fine example of a work in Expressionist style is Berg's three-act opera ***Wozzeck*** (1917–22). Wozzeck, a poor soldier, has allowed himself to be used for medical experiments which have crazed his mind. Marie, his mistress, has had a child by him, but is now attracted to a handsome Drum Major. Wozzeck, wild with jealousy, murders Marie beside a pond in the forest. Later, as he wades in to retrieve the knife, his insane mind imagines that the moon is bloody, that the pond is of blood. He flounders, and drowns . . .

Recorded on the cassette are two excerpts from *Wozzeck*. As you listen to the first (from Act 1, Scene 3) follow the translation on the next page.

[*Marie's room. Evening. A military band is coming down the street.*
Marie stands at the open window, her child in her arms]

Marie: [*speaking*] Tschin, Boom!
                 Tschin, Boom, Boom, Boom, Boom!
                 Hear, boy? They're coming now!

Margret: [*outside the window, speaking to Marie*]
                 What a man! Like a tree!

Marie: He marches just as proudly as a lion.
                 [*The Drum Major greets Marie. She waves to him*]

Margret: Why, what friendly warm looks, good neighbour!
                 It's seldom we get that from you!

Marie: [*singing*] Soldiers, O soldiers
                 are handsome fellows!

[*They squabble, then shriek at each other, as the band passes*]

Marie: [*shrieking*] Hussy!
                 [*she slams the window, shutting out the band music*]
                 Come, my boy. Let's ignore her slanders!
                 You're just a poor harlot's child,
                 but you give your mother, oh, so much joy
                 with your dear face that's never been blessed!
                 [*she rocks the child*]

Lul- la - by, ba - by . . .   Come, girl, what shall you do now?

You have a child but no man!   Why, what more could I ask?

Sing - ing to you ev' - ry night: Lul - la - by, ba - by, my

sweet - est boy.   No one to care   what we do!

Hansel, go harness your horses now,
give them good fodder today.
Give them no oats to eat,
no water shall they drink,
clearest, coolest wine must it be . . .
[*the child has fallen asleep*]
Clearest, coolest wine must it be!
[*Marie sinks deep into thought . . .*]

Assignment 83   Listen to the excerpt from *Wozzeck* two or three times more.

(a) During the first part of the excerpt, what features are there in the music which make it sound like a military band playing?

(b) When Marie slams the window shut, the music suddenly becomes very different. In what ways?

(c) As Marie sings her child to sleep, how does Berg make the music sound like a lullaby?

(d) The lullaby melody of bars 380–3 is heard again later on. At which words in the translation does it reappear?

(e) In the orchestral music which closes the excerpt, does Berg keep the same mood, or does he change it? How?

(f) Berg's music is basically atonal (without tonality, or key). Yet there are times, in the melodic line printed opposite, when the notes outline recognizable chords in the major-minor tonal system. Mention three instances where this occurs, giving bar numbers, and naming the chords.

Assignment 84   1 Listen to another excerpt from Berg's opera *Wozzeck*. The scene is a lonely forest path beside a pond. Dusk is falling. Wozzeck, insane and wild with jealousy, stabs Marie to death.

2 Listen to both these excerpts again. Which, do you think, is the most intensely and vividly 'Expressionistic'? In what ways?

Electronic music

Many composers since the 1950s (Stockhausen in particular) have explored the exciting possibilities of electronic music. An electronic composition may be made up entirely of electronically generated sounds – which may be pre-recorded on tape, or manipulated 'live' in the concert hall. Or a composer may combine electronic sounds with instruments or voices, sounding naturally or electronically modified, live or on tape.

Listen to two excerpts from a composition called **The Transistor Radio of St Narcissus** (1982–83) by the English composer Tim Souster, who has had close contact with Stockhausen, as student, performer, and assistant. The work requires two players. The music is for flugelhorn (player 1), pre-recorded tape and live electronics (player 2). The score consists of a part (in B♭) for the flugelhorn, and a graphic representation of the tape part. Player 2 is responsible for the amplification of the entire work, and also, at various times, uses electronics to modify the sounds of the 'live' flugelhorn by means of digital transposition and digital delay.

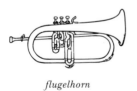

flugelhorn

When digital transposition is used, notes sounded by the flugelhorn are electronically *duplicated* at a higher or lower pitch, as required – the result giving the impression that there are *two* flugelhorns playing in parallel intervals (e.g. 5ths, or 4ths, or minor 3rds). Digital delay causes sounds to echo – repeating as they die away.

Assignment 85   The music of the first excerpt is printed on the next two pages. As the extract begins, the flugelhorn player is using a straight mute and is following a direction to improvise, imitating the sounds on the tape, while player 2 is electronically modifying the flugelhorn's sounds.

Look through the score, investigating the graphic representation of the tape part, and the flugelhorn part. Then listen to the music two or three times – matching sounds to printed signs, symbols, notes, and graphics.

Assignment 86 (a) Describe how any parts of this excerpt are examples of *aleatory* music (depending upon 'chance' or 'choice').

(b) What features are there in this music which definitely identify it as belonging to the 20th century?

🔊 **89** Now listen to another excerpt. This is the *coda*, which ends the piece. You will hear clear instances of digital transposition and digital delay; and also electronic imitations of 'morse', and of certain percussion instruments: low gong, snare drum, and hi-hat.

Assignment 87 (a) In the second excerpt from *The Transistor Radio of St Narcissus*, is the time signature $\frac{3}{4}$, $\frac{4}{4}$, $\frac{5}{4}$, or $\frac{6}{8}$?

(b) A melodic idea is repeated again and again in the bass. How many notes make up this idea?

(c) What is the name given to this particular musical device – in which a musical pattern is persistently and continuously repeated?

Assignment 88 Listen again to both excerpts from *The Transistor Radio of St Narcissus*.
In what ways are these two excerpts of music different from each other?

Jazz   An important type of music during the 20th century has been **jazz**, which originated in the southern states of the USA. Early jazz was usually played by a small band – the players improvising together, on and around a chosen melody, above a repeating pattern of chords. Among the main characteristics were a melodic style derived from the blues spiced with the syncopated rhythms of ragtime above a steady beat in $\frac{4}{4}$ time.

Listen to *At the Jazz Band Ball*, recorded by **Bix Beiderbecke and his Gang** in 1927. The music is based on this 32-bar chord pattern, which is in two sections, A and B:

1 Gm ⟶	2	3	4	5 F^7	6 B♭	7 C^7	8 F^7 D^7
9 Gm ⟶	10	11	12	13 C ⟶	14	15	16 F^7

17 G (major) ⟶	18	19 C ⟶	20	21 F^7 ⟶	22	23 B♭ ⟶	24
25 G ⟶	26	27 C	28 C^7	29 E♭ Edim	30 B♭$(^6_4)$ G^7	31 C^7 F^7	32 B♭

Bix Beiderbecke

Here is an outline plan of the piece, which is made up of six choruses:

Chorus 1:	A }	ensemble, in collective improvisation – with cornet
	B }	(Bix Beiderbecke) to the fore
Chorus 2:	A }	ensemble, in collective improvisation
	B }	
Chorus 3:	A	solo 1
	B	solo 2
Chorus 4:		solo 3 – 16 bars only
Chorus 5:		ensemble, in collective improvisation – 16 bars only
Chorus 6:		ensemble – 16 bars only (plus 1-bar coda)

Assignment 89   1 Play, or listen as your teacher plays, the 32-bar chord pattern on which *At the Jazz Band Ball* is based.

Q.O 90   2 Listen to the recording, following the outline plan above.

Assignment 90   Listen to *At the Jazz Band Ball* two or three times more.
1 (a) How many beats to a bar are there in this music?
  (b) Seven players made this recording. One plays cornet (Bix Beiderbecke). Another plays bass saxophone. What do the others play?
  (c) Describe the general mood of this music.
2 (a) During chorus 2, the bass saxophone improvises a brief unaccompanied solo. Is this called: a riff, a break, a bridge, or a coda?
  (b) Name the instruments which, in turn, play solos 1, 2, and 3.
3 Listen again to choruses 4, 5 and 6. Each is only 16 bars long. On which section of the chord pattern – A, or B – is each one based?

Fingerprints of musical style

Some characteristic features found in 20th-century music

Melodies are often short and fragmentary rather than long and winding – angular and spiky, including wide leaps with chromatic and dissonant intervals; glissandos ('slidings' from one pitch to another) or microtones (intervals smaller than a semitone) may be used; in some pieces, the ingredient of melody may be of secondary importance – or even be totally lacking.

Harmonies are likely to include a greater proportion of discords to concords – perhaps extreme dissonances (in some pieces, concords may be avoided altogether); note-clusters may be used (adjacent notes sounded together); the music may be polytonal (in two, or more, keys at the same time), or atonal (with no sense of tonality, or key).

Rhythms tend to be vigorous and dynamic, with frequent use of syncopation; unusual metres may be used, such as five or seven beats to a bar (often rooted in folk music); changes of metre from bar to bar; also polyrhythms (see page 12), ostinato devices ('obstinately' repeating), and energetic driving 'motor rhythms'.

Timbres are likely to claim attention – unusual combinations of timbres, expansion of the percussion section and more emphasis on percussive sounds in general, the inclusion of strange, intriguing and exotic sounds, striking (sometimes explosive) contrasts, and totally new sounds such as those involving electronic apparatus and magnetic tape; unfamiliar sounds from familiar instruments, e.g. instruments played at the extremes of their ranges, muted brass effects, new sounds from string instruments such as bowing behind the bridge, or tapping or striking the instrument with the fingertips or the bow, and new effects from wind instruments such as noisy key-clicking or valve-fingering, or playing on the detached mouthpiece; whispering, speaking, singing or shouting into an instrument; new effects and unusual uses of the human voice.

Making musical connections

Improvisation, which is such an important feature of jazz and blues, has always played an essential part in the music of India. There are two main traditions in Indian music: Hindustani, of north India (and including also Pakistan and Bangladesh); and Carnatic, of south India.

Most Indian classical music consists of three main elements:

- melody – often highly decorated with ornaments and nuances (shadings) of pitch;
- a rhythmic accompaniment, based on a repeating rhythm cycle called a *tala*;
- a drone.

Every performance consists largely, sometimes entirely, of improvisation, and is based upon a selected *raga*. A raga is not quite a scale, nor a mode, nor a melody – yet it has something in common with all three. It is, rather, an array of melodic materials which may be used to create a particular composition.

Each raga has an ascending form and a descending form. These may differ, so that during performance, melodic phrases which rise use the pitches of the ascending form, and melodic phrases which move downwards use those of the descending form. Each raga is associated with a particular mood or emotion; and, properly, should be performed at a specific time of day or night (e.g. dawn, noon, evening, after sunset, midnight).

Investigate an excerpt from a piece in the Carnatic tradition, called **Janani Mamava**. It is performed on typical south Indian instruments: two *vīnās*, and a *mṛdaṅgam*. The *vīnā* (one of the oldest string instruments) has seven strings, plucked with a wire plectrum. Four of them are melody strings; the other three are used as drone strings, and to accent the rhythms. The *mṛdaṅgam* is a double-headed barrel drum. It is played, with the hands, at both ends and combines treble and bass drums in a single instrument.

Sivasakthy Sivanesan playing the vīnā and Bhavani Shankar playing the mṛdaṅgam

92

☉☉ 91   The music is based on the raga *bhairavī*:

☉☉ 92   In this performance, the tala (which you have already encountered in the section on rhythm in chapter 1) is the *miśra cāpu*. This tala has beats grouped in sevens, and its cycle is 28 beats long.

☉☉ 93   Listen now to the excerpt from *Janani Mamava*. You will hear the last nine minutes or so of this 20-minute piece.

Assignment 91

(a) How is the drone effect created in this music?

(b) Do you notice any sections of music clearly repeated – or does the music seem to unfold continuously, freely and spontaneously?

(c) Describe the main changes you hear, in the sounds and the character of the music, during this excerpt from *Janani Mamava*.

Assignment 92

Listen to George Harrison's song '**Within you, without you**', from the album *Sergeant Pepper's Lonely Hearts' Club Band* by **The Beatles**. This song includes various sounds and ingredients from Indian music. First you will hear a drone on *tamburā*, a long-necked instrument with four strings which are strummed slowly and gently, one after another. And then the pitches of a scale are elaborated on a *dilrubā*, a bowed instrument with four melody strings and many sympathetic strings.

A rhythm set up on *tablā*, a pair of hand-played drums, leads into the first verse. Here is a skeleton plan of the song:

Introduction
Verse 1
Instrumental interlude
Verse 2

As you listen to the song, add as much detail as you can to the above plan – noting down interesting sounds and features which occur.

Assignment 93

Listen also to some of the following:

A raga* performed on sitar, tablā, and tamburā

Indian film music, such as *Pather Panchali**, or *Des Perdes*

Ravi Shankar: *Fire Night** – an 'experiment in combining jazz with Indian melodic and rhythmic elements'

A record of Hindi pop music, blending Eastern and Western styles

The Rolling Stones: 'Paint it Black' (including the sound of the sitar)

John Mayer (India/England): *Shanta Quintet* for sitar and strings (especially the last four minutes or so)

[* Included on *Ravi Shankar Improvisations*: Liberty LBL 83076E, or EMI EALP 1288]

Investigate an excerpt from **Symphony No. 6 for two orchestras** (1969) by the German composer, Hans Werner Henze. 'Two orchestras, with approximately equal resources, play together and in opposition, create echoes, canons, mirror images, variants and contrasts.' You will hear many colourful and varied timbres, and there are also some unusual playing techniques which create unusual sounds from familiar instruments.

Both orchestras contain a string section, and varied wind and percussion. Orchestra 1 (on the left) also has piano, harp, vibraphone, and guitar with contact microphone. Orchestra 2 (right) has electric organ, kettle drums, marimba, tom-toms, and violin with contact microphone.

Unusual playing techniques include: strings – tapping on the body of the instrument with the fingertips, bowing between the bridge and the tailpiece; wind – sounding indeterminate notes by using the mouthpiece only; keyboards – depressing keys with the flat of the hand, fist, or forearm. At times, players sound their highest possible (indeterminate) notes; and pianist and harpist stroke the strings with a brush.

Cuban son *rhythm:*

The music is a mix of 'classical' and folk style. The entire work is based, as far as rhythm is concerned, on ingredients from Latin-American folk music. Twice during the excerpt you will hear various Latin-American percussion instruments improvising freely on the Cuban *son* – a folk song and dance style based on a syncopated rhythm.

The Symphony includes certain aleatory ('chance–choice') elements. These include: sets of pitched notes to be repeated, but with players varying the order, or improvising the rhythm; groups of notes with durations given, but only the approximate pitches; sets of notes to be repeated but in each player's own time, or at differently marked *tempi* (speeds); also, the free improvisations on the Cuban *son*.

Occasionally, microtones are written in the string parts – the performers instructed to play certain notes a quarter-tone higher or lower.

94 Assignment 94

1 Listen to the final five minutes or so of the Symphony. Follow the chart opposite which shows, with approximate elapsed timing, how the music divides into seven sections. Some details are given for sections 1 to 5.
2 Listen again, and complete the chart by adding details of unusual sounds and interesting events and features which you notice in sections 6 and 7.

> "Music is my secret world."
>
> "Composing is like digging for gems in a rich mine-shaft. The mine-shaft is your own soul..."
>
> (Hans Werner Henze)

Section	Some sounds and features to listen for . . .
1 (0' 00")	A build-up of tension – then powerful brass *glissandi* ('slidings'), spiky *staccato* texture with some string instruments played *col legno* (the strings beaten with the wood of the bow) and some wind instruments playing their highest possible sounds. Listen also for piano 'splashes', and for steel sheets to be shaken.
2 (0' 49")	Electric violin, excited, rising; snare drum, forceful, with *col legno* strings . . . A high, strident note-cluster – held, then released.
3 (1' 21")	First improvisation on the Cuban *son*, *pp*, on percussion: bongos, cowbell in orchestra 1, and kettle drums, maraca, güiro in orchestra 2 – all against a quiet, sustained background.
4 (1' 57")	An aggressive outburst on the opposed brass of both orchestras – then kettle drums prominent, leading to:
5 (2' 10")	Second improvisation on the Cuban *son*, *fff* – while instruments of both orchestras, rapidly and individually, repeat patterns of different pitches, creating a dense and intricate background texture.
6 (2' 37")	A brief pause – then . . .
7 (3' 56")	A reference to the syncopated rhythm of the Cuban *son*; then . . .

Assignment 95   Improvising on a rhythm

1 Form a group of four musicians – three choosing percussion instruments, the fourth using voice or a melodic instrument. Select one of these Latin-American dance rhythms:

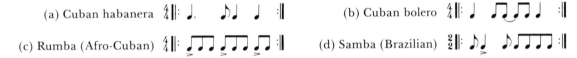

(a) Cuban habanera   (b) Cuban bolero

(c) Rumba (Afro-Cuban)   (d) Samba (Brazilian)

Player 1 begins by steadily repeating the basic dance rhythm.
Player 2 joins in by repeating a pattern which picks out (emphasizes) only certain notes or beats.
Player 3 joins in and improvises rhythmically and freely, using patterns which include swifter notes – and perhaps also rests, and syncopations.
Player 4 joins in by improvising melodic phrases, riffs, or a complete melody (perhaps slow-moving) floating above the rhythmic accompaniment.

Record your piece; then listen to it and discuss it. (Are the timbres effective enough? Are the dynamics and the balance correct?)

2 Try another piece, swapping parts. Use either the same basic rhythm, or a different one.

Assignment 96   Compose a short piece for a small group of varied instruments. Include some of the unusual sounds and playing techniques used by Henze in his Symphony No. 6 – and also discover/create some of your own. Carefully work out how you can notate your ideas, clearly, for the players.

Some features in the general style of much 20th-century music may be traced back to influences from American jazz. For example:

- a fresh vitality in the rhythm, often with strong syncopations;
- syncopated melodies, sometimes with 'blue' notes – flattening certain notes of the scale such as the 3rd or 7th;
- muted brass effects, a keener interest in percussive sounds, and instruments playing in shrill registers.

◯◯ 95 **Assignment 97** Listen to a dance from the ballet ***La Création du Monde*** by Milhaud. He composed it in 1923 after hearing black jazz musicians performing in New York, and in the music he deliberately included features from jazz.
(a) Name the first five instruments which, in turn, play the opening tune.
(b) On which of these musical devices does the structure of the music rely?

    riff;   break;   ostinato;   fugato.

(c) Which sounds and ingredients from jazz do you hear in this music?

Assignment 98 Listen to 'One' (from the album . . . *And Justice For All*) by the San Francisco-based band **Metallica** who, in the late 1980s, 'took thrash metal to the masses'. Here is a basic plan of the first half of the song:

0′00″	Introduction:	sound effects ⟶ instruments
1′42″	Verse 1:	'I can't remember anything . . .'
2′16″	Interlude 1:	instruments
2′30″	Verse 2:	'Back in the womb . . .'
3′04″	Interlude 2:	instruments
3′31″	Verse 3 (short):	'Now the world has gone . . .'

1 (a) Identify the sound effects heard in the Introduction.
  (b) Name the first two instruments you hear. Describe the mood presented.
  (c) Which of these rhythms is repeated by the drummer?

(1) 4/4 rhythm   (2) 4/4 rhythm   (3) 4/4 rhythm

  (d) Does the metre remain 4/4 – or does it change?
  (e) In Interlude 1, is the musical material new – or has it been heard earlier on?
  (f) In Interlude 2, which instrument is featured mostly?

2 After Verse 3, listen on, and note down all the interesting features that you notice.

3 In an interview for TV, Lars Ulrich (drums, Metallica) commented: 'We have concentrated on an honest interpretation of some of the stuff of the real world, instead of trying to paint fake façades'. Listen to 'One' again.
  (a) What is the basic idea or message of the words of this song?
  (b) How does the music gradually come to reflect this more clearly during the second half of the song?
  (c) Imagine you are the producer for a Metallica concert. What lighting, and effects, would you use for this song?